LEARNING TO MANAGE

Other titles from IES:

Changing Roles for Senior Managers
Kettley P, Strebler M T
IES Report 327, 1997. ISBN 1-85184-255-1

Personal Feedback: Cases in Point
Kettley P
IES Report 326, 1997. ISBN 1-85184-254-3

Competence Based Management Training
Strebler M T, Bevan S
IES Report 302, 1996. ISBN 1-85184-228-4

A catalogue of these and over 100 other titles is available from IES.

LEARNING TO MANAGE

Other titles from IES:

Changing Roles for Senior Managers
Kettley P, Strebler M T
IES Report 327, 1997. ISBN 1-85184-255-1

Personal Feedback: Cases in Point
Kettley P
IES Report 326, 1997. ISBN 1-85184-254-3

Competence Based Management Training
Strebler M T, Bevan S
IES Report 302, 1996. ISBN 1-85184-228-4

A catalogue of these and over 100 other titles is available from IES.

the | **Institute**
for | **Employment**
Studies

LEARNING TO
MANAGE

P Tamkin
L Barber

A study supported by the
IES Research Club

Report 345

Published by:

THE INSTITUTE FOR EMPLOYMENT STUDIES
Mantell Building
University of Sussex
Brighton BN1 9RF
UK

Tel. + 44 (0) 1273 686751
Fax + 44 (0) 1273 690430

http://www.employment-studies.co.uk

British Cataloguing-in-Publication Data

A catalogue record for this publication is available from the British Library

ISBN 1-85184-273-X

Printed in Great Britain by Ikon Office Solutions plc

The Institute for Employment Studies

IES is an independent, international and apolitical centre of research and consultancy in human resource issues. It works closely with employers in the manufacturing, service and public sectors, government departments, agencies, professional and employee bodies, and foundations. Since it was established over 27 years ago the Institute has been a focus of knowledge and practical experience in employment and training policy, the operation of labour markets and human resource planning and development. IES is a not-for-profit organisation which has a multidisciplinary staff of over 50. IES expertise is available to all organisations through research, consultancy and publications.

IES aims to help bring about sustainable improvements in employment policy and human resource management. IES achieves this by increasing the understanding and improving the practice of key decision makers in policy bodies and employing organisations.

The IES Research Club

This report is the product of a study supported by the IES Research Club, through which a group of IES Corporate Members finance, and often participate in, applied research on employment issues. The members of the Club are:

BAA plc	Inland Revenue
Barclays Bank plc	Littlewoods Organisation plc
BBC	Lloyds TSB Group
British Steel plc	Marks & Spencer plc
BT plc	National Westminster Bank plc
Cabinet Office (OPS)	NHS Executive
Department of Health	Orange plc
DETR	Post Office
Electricity Association	Rolls-Royce plc
Glaxo Wellcome plc	J Sainsbury plc
Guardian Insurance	Shell UK Ltd
Halifax plc	Unilever UK (Holdings) Ltd
HM Customs & Excise	Woolwich Building Society

Acknowledgements

We would like to thank all the organisations who took part in this research for their co-operation and openness. We would also like to thank all those learners who took the time to speak to us about their learning experiences and their colleagues for their contribution.

Contents

Summary

Really good managers are in great demand and short supply. Organisations spend considerable sums of money training, educating and developing their management populations and yet organisations and their workforces still suffer autocratic bullies whose moment in organisational history has long gone. Worse than this are the far greater numbers of managers who have the potential to be really good but don't seem to quite realise what to do or who cannot find the time or motivation to do it differently. These are the managers who don't communicate fully, who lack the confidence, the ability or the empathy to coach people to better performance, who spend too much time in the escapism of expert 'doing' and too little in the front line of expert managing.

There would appear to be a crisis in British management, a sudden lack of confidence exacerbated by the changing demands of organisations. All those structural changes of the late 1980s and early 1990s have led to demands for managers who can empower their workforce to greater commitment and effort, who can create democratic and involved communities and who can form development partnerships with individuals to help them in the practice of lifelong learning.

This report looks at the learning experiences of managers in a number of organisations, of the ways in which they learn, of what they learn, of the impact this has on them and the impact this has on their organisations. We interviewed some sixty managers, their managers in turn and their subordinates from five organisations from both public and private sectors.

How do managers learn?

Managers learn in many different ways both formal and informal. They learn from job or role changes, from significant others, either implicitly when they act as role models, or explicitly in a coaching or mentoring relationship; they learn from formal courses or with the support of colleagues or peers.

What is surprising is not the variety of learning methods but the fact that most of our managers would acknowledge that they were not conscious learners. If managers are to learn from the day to day it has to be an experience 'big' enough to hit them between the eyes. For most managers being 'big' is synonymous with being unpleasant; the huge mistake, a personal tragedy, failing to cope. To learn best from everyday experience of a less traumatic kind requires some structure and support.

What do managers learn?

Our managers had learned many things from their learning experiences and these could be clustered into: knowledge; technical skills; management skills; increased understanding of their organisation; increased understanding of their impact on others and increased understanding of themselves.

What was clear was that what we learn is strongly influenced by how we learn. Those managers who had learned through formal taught courses had acquired knowledge and technical skills, those who had learned through networking with others either within their organisation or from other organisations had learned much more about their organisation, its structure, processes and culture. Those who had undergone a learning experience that involved personal feedback were much more likely to have learned something about themselves and their impact on others.

The impact of learning

It is one thing to learn something, it is quite another to make use of that learning, or for that learning to change behaviour in some way. The manager who has learnt that others see them as aggressive needs to use that learning to affect behaviour. Learning that remains hidden within the individual, that is not used to do the job differently or to impact on management style cannot affect the organisation or others within it.

This report presents clear examples of changing behaviours and styles of doing things. Some of these managers had undertaken an MBA programme that had involved much analysis of personal and cognitive style. As a result they showed change in a number of cognitive areas:

- strategic overview
- thinking style
- action orientation
- reflection.

Other managers demonstrated change in their personal style, their self awareness and their ways of dealing with others. These changes were frequently as a result of receiving feedback from peers and subordinates which some described as being of startling honesty. Through this feedback managers had reconsidered what was valued behaviour and reassessed their responses to others. The changes in them were fundamentally to do with internal censorship. They had either learnt to relax an internal censor that stopped them behaving in certain ways because of a belief that it was inappropriate, or to impose a censorship on behaviour that had been shown to be detrimental to them, for example:

- showing a more sensitive caring side of themselves that they had previously kept hidden
- toning down aggressive behaviour because of feedback of the impact it had on others.

Organisational impact

Trying to determine the effect that training and development has on an organisation is very hard work indeed, hence the proliferation of seminars, conferences and offers of consultancy to assist organisations make the link. When the development activities are designed to impact on the soft people skills of managers it is even more difficult to make any assessment of organisational outcome.

It is impossible to prove that the management development programmes that we studied have changed their organisations, but what was observed in the organisations that we looked at was organisational change that was culturally consistent with the style of the development activity. Thus these organisations had on the whole become more democratic, more open, less hierarchical, less patriarchal in their style and their interactions.

Key themes

Much of the learning and its impact on managerial behaviour centred around soft skills. This is of particular interest to organisations as previous research has shown that soft skills are becoming increasingly important in determining what makes a really good manager, and yet soft skills have proved hard to develop and hard to assess.

From all the information we have gathered and from all the people that we have spoken to there appear to emerge some key themes that help explain the changes in soft skills that managers report in themselves and which are, on the whole, confirmed by those around them.

The first step in creating really good managers is that they should first know themselves. Much management development focuses on the external world and the development of knowledge and skills that are 'out there' — understanding budgets, where business strategy comes from, what a good appraisal process should look like and so on. Really effective management develop-ment places considerable emphasis on the internal world. This development of the internal world focuses on both knowledge and skills — what are my strengths and weaknesses, how do I normally react when put under pressure, what techniques can I use to overcome my reluctance to deal with conflict.

Self knowledge is not that easy to come by; we tend to avoid situations that make us feel uncomfortable which can include potentially useful feedback. We also tend to be blind to the impact some of our characteristic behaviours have on others. Unfortunately, the more senior the manager the less likely they are to experience feedback or to be able to find the time for reflection. So understanding and knowing self requires some help to be given to the learner.

Two processes appear to be essential if individuals are to develop greater internal skills and knowledge: feedback opportunities and support mechanisms. Those that have received structured feedback within a supportive and trusting environment have used this to change themselves for the better, becoming more proactive, more self confident and more empathic in their dealings with others. Feedback can play a positive role in enhancing self esteem through increasing self knowledge.

However, feedback is not always welcomed. In an unsupported environment, feedback can be perceived as threatening when it tells the individual something they did not know about themselves, and are not ready to integrate into their self knowledge. In these circumstances a vicious circle is set up.

Support from those that the learner has come to trust appears to be crucial if feedback is to be warmly received. Once an individual has integrated such feedback into their self knowledge and accepted it, there would appear to be an increase in the value attached to feedback and the desire to seek it out.

Learning more about ourselves, and seeing ourselves more as others see us, enables us to deal with others with greater empathy and greater awareness of our impact. We can then confront our traditional ways of doing and thinking about things and begin to move in the direction that we desire. After all, this is what real development is all about.

1 The Link Between Individual and Organisational Learning

1.1 Introduction

The link between individual and organisational learning has been a key issue for academics and practitioners alike and has grown in popularity since debate on the Learning Organisation became more popular. In one sense organisational learning is something of a conundrum, as Argyris and Schon (1981) put it:

'What is an organisation that it may learn?'

It is very easy when dealing with something so intangible to get lost in a semantic muddle, wonder if the concept has any meaning whatsoever, and decide learning can only be about individuals who comprise the organisation. The depressing thing about this scenario is that the natural movement of individuals means that they take all that learning with them, to the organisation's loss.

Yet we all talk so easily about organisational culture, about the structures, systems, policies and processes that make one organisation different from another. We look to understand how one organisation might rise to success while another fades. We imbue organisations with all kinds of characteristics that might be hard to explain in words and yet we know what we mean. Moreover, when we analyse our concept of culture it is clear that this cannot be vested in individuals. Organisational culture is remarkably stable and notoriously difficult to change despite the movement of people in and out. If organisations can have a style, a way of doing things, a way of communicating and responding then why not a way of learning? And if organisational learning is not merely the sum of the parts of individual learning then what is the relationship between the learning of the individual and the learning of the organisation? How does learning transfer, how can we make the difference?

This research study set out to examine the links between individual and organisational learning. We wanted to know if the linkages were more likely to occur with certain kinds of development intervention than others; was there something about the development event itself, the numbers of people involved, its length, its approach. We chose to concentrate on this learning transfer in managers for a number of reasons: they are crucial to the success of organisations, frequently having more autonomy and freedom to act than more junior staff. We also know from a host of research studies that they receive more training and development within organisations than other staff groups (*eg* Gallie and White, 1993; Tremlett and Park, 1995; Metcalf *et al.*, 1994). They are also a group that has been attacked in the UK for being under-educated and under-performing (Handy, 1987; Constable and McCormick, 1987). If they are so crucial, it seems to make sense to look more carefully at the way they learn and see how this learning impacts on the organisation and makes a difference.

We also debated where we would place the focus of our enquiries. Learning is a wide concept encompassing training whether formal off-the-job, formal on-the-job or other less formal means, that may be interpreted differently by individuals (Campenelli, *et al.*, 1994). It can also include learning from experience, from others explicitly or implicitly, or from personal insight. With this potential array of possible research options we decided a more focused approach would yield greater insights. As a consequence we decided to concentrate on some kind of formal intervention designed to bring about individual or organisational learning. We appreciate that this approach could be criticised for possibly ignoring the other forms of development that are likely to encompass the vast majority of learning experiences, and so we also explored with individuals other forms of learning that they were aware of. But we needed to focus, and this focus needs to be on those areas of learning that the organisation can have some influence over. It may well be that individuals do most of their learning informally through observation and experience, but this is difficult stuff to influence. It is anarchic at best and leaves the organisation and indeed the individuals at the mercy of the experiences and role models that the organisation can offer. It is also reliant on the observance, sensitivity and readiness to learn of the individual. Self-observation would indicate that many of us sleep-walk past much that could furnish us with insight. The self-conscious learner is rare indeed and often has to be trained to develop and utilise the skill (Green and Gibbons, 1995; Harri-Augstein and Thomas, 1991). A reliance on an unreliable and amateur phenomenon is unlikely to cause the step change in management and organisational performance that we were seeking.

We were also intrigued by the notion of individual and organisational transformation, one of the ways that the learning organisation has been described (Pedlar *et al.*, 1991). How can individuals be transformed? How can organisations lever extraordinary performance out of ordinary resources (Towers, 1995)? How can organisations transform themselves and the way they operate? Such transformations surely require some kind of deliberate intervention. Can we possibly step change anything from within our existing mental models, our existing cultural frameworks? What is it that makes us configure our worlds differently, that makes us break the habits of a lifetime and actually do things differently? If it is anywhere, then the holy grail of management development lies here. Vast amounts of organisational money are spent on improving performance. When the performance is a skill such as using a new computer package or operating a new piece of equipment, then training and development can be shown to be moderately successful providing some well known rules are observed:

- that the learner is ready and able to learn
- that the training provided is suitable for the purpose, and the skill and aptitude of the learner
- that the opportunity to use the newly acquired skill will quickly follow the development experience.

When the skill is something as intangible as management skills, then organisations generally have a pretty poor track record of changing managerial behaviour. This difficulty has been brought into sharp relief by the experiences of organisations that have responded to the pressures brought by the recession and increasing competitiveness. The responses of many have become all too familiar, with downsizing, delayering and flattening management hierarchies commonplace. As a consequence, management style has also had to change, with the shift towards more sharing of control and responsibility within organisations. With fewer managers co-ordinating larger areas, a controlling, dictatorial management style is impossibly hard work. Empowerment may be trendy but it also makes good business sense. In the same way that retail and catering have moved to become more self-service — getting the customer to do more of the work, so organisations have moved towards making the workers more self-managing and therefore enabling the organisation to survive and prosper with fewer managers.

To summarise we decided to concentrate on:

- deliberate intervention programmes to see what lessons there are for other organisations that seek to make a difference
- a management population, because it is here that organisations have traditionally allocated the bulk of their resources and it is in this population that individuals have greatest freedom to act.
- what makes the difference, what has the power to change the ways individuals behave, and possibly the ways organisations operate.

1.2 Approach

Our research was conducted using a case study approach involving five well known organisations. We asked these organisations to allow us to speak to approximately ten individuals that had recently participated in a formal management development programme. We also interviewed those from the human resource (HR) function who were involved in employee development and could comment on the organisation's approach and current initiatives. As well as interviewing individuals who had been through the programme, we attempted to interview some subordinates to gain their perspective on the impact of the development of their managers, and also some more senior managers who could comment on the development from a senior perspective. In essence we were trying to create a 360 degree view of the impact of the development programme and of other forms of development. The focus of the interview was on individual development in the widest sense and then narrowing down to the impact of the particular management development event or other events that had been of particular importance. All interviews were conducted using a semi-structured interview guide (Appendix 1).

The participating companies were:

- Marks and Spencer plc
- The Post Office
- a government department
- The Open University
- Sainsbury's Supermarkets Ltd

2 The Meaning of the 'Learning Organisation'

The debate on individual and organisational learning is grounded in the concept of the 'learning organisation' but despite its popularity, the concept of the learning organisation is surrounded by semantic muddle. On the surface it seems a seductive and believable notion; the idea that organisations should aspire to the ability to recognise changes in their environment, that they should be able to learn from their actions and both adapt to environmental change and become better at doing so. Scratching below the surface reveals a confusion as to exactly what the concept means and what a learning organisation might look like in practice.

Much of the criticism levelled at the learning organisation concept has revolved around this lack of clarity over meaning and the difficulty of translating the concept into action. In this chapter we seek to unravel the concept by looking critically at what has been said about it.

2.1 Definition

The term 'learning organisation' was first coined by Pedlar et al., 1988 in the UK, and by Hayes et al., 1988 in the US. Pedlar et al's definition centred on organisational transformation through the learning of an organisation's members. Despite the fact that the term has been in circulation for some time, tying down the definition of the concept has proved to be a difficult task. Descriptions of a learning organisation are numerous and vary in tone. Many are clearly Utopian, such as that given by Senge (1990):

'Where people continually expand their capacity to create the results they truly desire, where new and expansive patterns of thinking are nurtured, where collective aspiration is set free, and where people are continually learning how to learn together.'

Many others have stressed the importance of learning and change within the definition, for example Kremer-Bennett and O'Brien (1994):

'It's an organisation that has woven a continuous and enhanced capacity to learn, adapt and change into its culture.'

Little wonder that such definitions have caused frustration amongst those that seek to understand the concept in terms of its practical application rather than as an intellectual exercise. In a deliberate attempt to move away from such esoteric definitions Garvin (1993) offers:

'A learning organisation is an organisation skilled at creating, acquiring, and transferring knowledge, and at modifying its behaviour to reflect new knowledge and insights.'

There are certain recurring themes in the definitions that can be teased out. For example, there is a central theme of learning, indeed there has been considerable debate just on this part of the concept alone. The consensus seems to be that this learning is not just of individuals but of the organisation itself and that this 'whole' is greater than the sum of the individual parts. The other recurring theme is that of change.

2.2 Individual learning

Some of the most interesting concepts within the literature of the learning organisation treat adult learning as more than a single entity. Learning is seen as encompassing different levels of functioning and with different impact on both the individual and the organisation. One of the most useful models here is that proposed by Argyris and Schon (1974, 1978, 1981) of single and double loop learning. Single loop learning is learning how to do something better within an existing system or framework, double loop learning involves the challenging and changing of the system or framework. The concepts are similar to the ideas of Revens (1982); programmed learning adds to the sum of knowledge where questioning learning reorganises it.

In a remarkably similar way, Kim (1993) writes of learning encompassing know-how and know-why, which can be defined as 'increasing one's capacity to take effective action'. Torbert (1991) is another commentator who has expanded the concepts of single and double loop learning further with the addition of the concept of triple loop learning. Triple loop learning challenges the entire rationale of the organisation within which the system or framework operates.

These ideas of learning occurring at different levels, with greater value being ascribed to levels of learning that are in some way deemed to be higher or deeper, has also been subscribed to elsewhere. For example, Bateson (1987) coined the phrase of 'deutero-learning' for the goal of learning to learn and becoming more skilled at problem solving. On a more esoteric note, Senge's concept of personal mastery (1990), is defined as the individual developing his/her learning through the creative tension of vision and reality. This involves methods such as meditation, imagery and visualisation. Torbert (1991 and 1994) argues that higher stages of individual development lead to better performance, and the ability to take on more complex problems and to make the links between issues. This strikes a chord with the systems thinking described by Senge.

These higher levels of consciousness are characterised by independence, self-actualisation, broadened awareness, capacity for love, empathy, creativity, spontaneity and inspiration. Separate from the literature concerned with the levels of learning there is another body of writing that concentrates on the methods of learning. This has a long history and stems from the ideas of Reg Revens' concept of action learning (1982). This deceptively simple idea, that individuals learn better by doing, has gained considerable credibility and Revens' ideas have formed a mainstay of much development literature. Knowles (1989) is another who has argued that adults learn most through experience, self-directed learning and by means of actual day-to-day jobs and routines. Adult learning is characterised by personal autonomy, experiential learning, and connection and meaning being made.

Taking a completely different approach to most of the literature on participation and individual benefits to learning, this research and academic writing can be summarised as a belief that all learning is not equal. There are more complex kinds of learning that are potentially of greater use to individuals and organisations, that are more likely to transform the learner and which are more likely to lead to the most desired of human behaviours such as creativity and inspiration.

Whatever the level of learning, it is more likely to be effective if embedded in the day-to-day context than it is through formal training or education.

2.3 Organisational learning

Pedlar *et al.* (1991) have stressed that individual learning is a necessary pre-requisite of organisational learning but is not by itself enough. Understanding individual learning is vital to the learning organisation, but it is also necessary to understand how this individual learning can be translated into organisational learning. There is a conceptual problem here that is beautifully put by Argyris and Schon (1978):

> *'There is something paradoxical here. Organisations are not merely collections of individuals, yet there are no organisations without such collections. Similarly, organisational learning is not merely individual learning, yet organisations learn only through the experiences and actions of individuals. What then are we to make of organisational learning? What is an organisation that it may learn?'*

In answering this issue many have used similar concepts to those developed to explain individual learning, so the concepts of single and double loop learning have been applied to organisations as if they were individuals.

The single and double loop learning models of Argyris and Schon have been interpreted by some by describing mental models, *ie* the ways individuals and companies construe the world which, in turn, affects their perceptions and actions.

The action learning concepts have also gained organisational currency, for example Pettigrew and Whipp (1991) focus on organisational capability — the hidden learning that takes place which informs and influences what happens.

The higher levels of learning that have been proposed in an individual capacity have also had an impact at an organisational level. Jones and Hendry (1994) believe that the development of a learning organisation will result in individuals asking questions of an ethical, moral and personal kind, related to the purpose of work and the nature of society. They believe that the learning organisation brings hard and soft learning (*ie* learning in social contexts) together, and in doing so causes stress and disruption for both individual and the organisation. Senge believes (1990), that this shift in mind attitudes and perceptions, his concept of 'metanoia' is necessary to help organisations see and think more clearly.

Many of the concepts that have been applied to individual learning have been adapted also to explain organisational learning. These have included the single and double loop learning models of Argyris and Schon. The concept of action learning has equal validity in the organisational as well as the individual context, and there is a body of literature that stresses the importance of the emotional context of learning as well as its level and context. The message seems to be that learning impacts on individuals and their organisations in many different ways. The potential of learning to transform is not the result of training and development *per se* but the acquisition of critical powers to challenge the status quo.

Garvin (1993) describes learning organisations as being skilled at five main activities:

- systematic problem solving
- experimentation
- learning from past experience, *ie* systematically reviewing past successes and failures
- learning from others through the adoption of techniques such as benchmarking
- transferring knowledge through information flows and education.

Torbert (1994) has written about the barriers to developing simultaneous individual and managerial learning. In his view:

- According to development theory only those at higher levels of development can possibly appreciate the benefits of developing others to such levels, therefore in many organisations no-one will be committed to the process.
- The development of others requires a non-coercive, but confrontational style which few people routinely demonstrate.

- There is nothing that will routinely cause organisational learning.
- The type of organisational structure that will integrate individual and organisational learning is not known.

This viewpoint is uniquely pessimistic about the difficulties of becoming a learning organisation, which, given what we do know of cultural change may also be uniquely realistic.

2.4 Conclusion

The literature on the learning organisation has been analysed and found to separate broadly into a limited number of main areas. There is an element which concentrates on individual learning as the key concept. This describes how individuals learn, and the levels of learning that are possible.

Another body of literature concentrates on the link between individual and organisational learning and in the main finds that the same concepts remain applicable and robust in the organisational context. What is lacking in the published literature is similar to that which is lacking in the literature on the organisational outcomes of learning; there is very little hard evidence on the benefits of the process to persuade any cynics to place their faith and their resources in its attainment. What the literature does provide is a reminder that searching for the positive benefits of learning is bound to be clouded by the fact that we are not dealing with a single concept. Not all training and development is equal; teaching an individual to do a particular task better may not impact on the way they do other tasks. As Ryan (in Hirsh and Wagner, 1993) pointed out, the quality of the training and development will affect the outcome.

Marks and Spencer plc

Background

Marks and Spencer, one of the UK's best known organisations, has been consistently considered one of the most successful and well managed organisations in our economy. The background to the introduction of the management development programmes that were the focus of our visit, was a time of massive change. The organisation was looking to improve and wanted to explore solutions that were not specifically academic but highly pragmatic in nature. There was a clear focus on priorities with the organisation looking for business value. The organisation was trying to embed learning into the culture, getting all staff to understand that learning is something that happens all the time. This message is delivered both directly and subliminally through vehicles such as the in-house staff magazine. The organisation has a very informal management and communication style with a low emphasis on paper communication. For these reasons the organisation does not have formal written mission statements. It was described to us as a very intuitive business with individuals learning through networking.

The development context

Marks and Spencer (M&S) runs a range of management development programmes covering junior to very senior management grades. These programmes have a certain commonality of approach and philosophy that was unique amongst those organisations that we spoke to. The approach is one of challenge and assessment, of feedback and confrontation, of opening up and sharing. This makes the development programmes a daring change from the more usual and safe knowledge based management development. They seem to be part of a higher risk strategy; and with much that has a high risk associated, the possible impacts of failure are greater and the possible benefits to the organisation are greater still. We looked at individuals who had attended two development programmes: a middle management development programme and a senior management development programme. Both populations had also experienced other forms of management development which were also mentioned, and like all the individual learners that we spoke to, other learning events had also been important for them. These included the impact of other people, changing personal circumstances, and new jobs that had stretched them beyond their existing boundaries.

Despite its enviable position at the top of the UK's organisations as judged by peers, the organisation has been open to learning from others as well as from the variety of practice that can be provided within the organisation. Approximately five years ago the organisation explored the options with business schools of a formal consortium programme based on action learning and benchmarking. The programme had top level support in M&S and four other organisations. These organisations were deliberately chosen from non-competing industries but had to be industry leaders. Each organisation places five participants who follow five themes in five modules. Each module takes two and a half days over six months with participants working in cross-company teams visiting each company. The consortium has been immensely successful and has been viewed as a powerful learning experience by all those that have participated. Such has been the success in M&S that a consortium programme has been developed for the next level down, using internal benchmarking. Some of the key learning outcomes have been seen to be leadership skills, leadership style and globalisation. There has been greater awareness of the benefits of allowing individuals greater scope and the opportunities to take risks.

Interestingly, all the individuals we spoke to who had been on the consortium project also mentioned two earlier experiences of management development programmes within M&S. The first was a consultant-led management development programme with an emphasis on team building, bonding and opening up. The programme was highly personal with some experiencing a fairly rough ride. This was followed some time later by the Senior Management Development Programme which was led by the Chief Executive of M&S. Whilst also not being afraid to deal with the personal side of managerial life, this programme emphasised the building of networks more and the business focus was sharper. There was still a strong emphasis on feedback of strengths and weaknesses, and the building of those that attended into a team, utilising an open and honest communication style.

For middle managers a similar programme was run, called the Management Development Programme (MDP). This adopted a similar style to the senior programme and was indeed developed and run with the same consultancy. Once again the emphasis is on feedback from peers, managers and subordinates that challenges traditional styles of behaving and acting. The programmes deliberately create close support groups amongst programme participants, many of which go on to form an action learning set to give ongoing peer support. Further support is provided through a cohort mentor who helps facilitate sets getting together and acts as another learning resource.

The Post Office

Background

The Post Office and its constituent businesses, are a hugely successful publicly owned business. With the breakup and privatisation of much that was in public ownership, The Post Office is the largest and most successful public utility. The business currently makes a profit of some £577m per year that feeds into the Treasury budget. Despite its success, the organisation has still been subject to massive change pressures which culminated with a failed privatisation attempt in 1995. However, with the change in government the debate on status continues. The culture has changed significantly over the years from a highly unionised bureaucracy to a modern business which has become steadily less blame-centred, moving towards a less authoritarian management style that encourages continuous development, empowerment and coaching. In order to sustain competitive advantage the organisation has recently initiated a strategic agenda to address four key issues: Technology, People, Product Development and Overheads.

The development context

The business has adopted a tiered management development approach that provides tailored development for all levels in the organisation. The Senior Management Development Architecture is operated centrally for the most senior managers in the Post Office. Each of the constituent business/group wide schemes supplements this for those below the most senior level. This architecture provides:

- High level workshops 'the Business Leaders Seminars' are provided for the top 50 that deal with live and emerging corporate issues. These seminars are focused on strategy and generate strategic projects which feed into the business plans.

- For the 200 senior managers, the 'Business Management Programme' (BMP) focuses on high fliers or those earmarked as having particular talent, providing presentations from internal and external experts. Participants complete project work as part of the programme, which may be utilised by the business.

- For the bulk of senior managers (some 1,500) there is a variety of management development programmes, one of which is an MBA type programme.

- In addition to the above there are development workshops that fit in between these programmes.

These workshops are designed for individuals and their bosses and are externally facilitated. They are designed to generate personal awareness and lead to the production of a personal development plan which is monitored by the individual's line manager and HR. Separately from these formal programmes designed to reach a particular target population, there are management development initiatives that are more exclusive and more personal in their focus.

There is an attempt to promote a learning culture within the business but there are still many barriers to this. Up until recently the separate sub-businesses were encouraged to operate independently, partly as a preparation for what seemed a likely privatisation. When privatisation did not take place, the organisation has had to rethink this strategy. The corporate centre has become proactive in developing common standards, values and behaviours to create a more cohesive culture, and to encourage business-wide learning and support.

Government Department

Background

The Civil Service generally has been pursuing a process of increasing devolution to departments and units within departments. In some cases this has been formally recognised through agency status, and even in others there has been growing recognition of unit and departmental autonomy with the devolution of pay and grading authorities. The consequences of such change for the Government Department, like many others, has been change on a massive scale. Departments that were once part of a much larger whole, where much HR policy was determined centrally, found themselves having to cope with local responsibility and autonomy. This was coupled with increasing public sector budgetary strictures which meant staff reductions needed to be both managed and responded to in the staffing of personnel units. The consequence of this was doing more with less, which has led individual departments to devolve more to the line.

Alongside these changes the role of the HR function is changing to being more facilitative, while much of their previous responsibilities are undertaken by the line. In our Government Department this theme of devolution has been occurring for some time.

The development context

The training and development ethos is one where individuals are responsible for their own development, enabled and supported by the line manager and a small HR team at the centre. This relationship is made explicit through a brochure entitled 'Developing Your Skills' distributed to all staff. Other initiatives have included a new appraisal system that cascades objective setting so that everyone can understand their part in the strategic picture. They have also just introduced a core competency framework to which training and development is in the process of being aligned. The line is responsible for preparing a strategic development plan (by unit heads).

It is hoped that the new performance management system will increase demand for development, as it is very development focused. As the scheme also drives performance related pay, it remains to be seen if this will impact on the outcome. This devolvement to the line is still in the early stages and is inhibited for the moment by the line being reluctant to test the market and therefore defaulting to internal courses.

Corporate HR is benchmarking development activity against a number of well known private sector examples. For instance, the department has set up a learning resource centre, including an employee development centre where individuals can assess themselves using development centre techniques. The department has just introduced succession planning and open advert.

Policy could be described as consisting of a pick and mix approach; there are a variety of courses aimed at administration staff to enhance their job-related skills such as letter writing, numeracy *etc*. There are also a number of management modules aimed at particular skill needs such as dealing with conflict, mentoring, learning to listen. The style of these events is highly participative and includes syndicate work, working through case studies and learning from each other. These initiatives are not at present thoroughly evaluated, although the department is participating in an evaluation programme with a university. At present there is no evaluation of on-the-job training, and projects and secondments are rarely used. The core training programme represents the minority of the training budget.

The Open University

Background

In 1993 the Open University began a major change programme in support of its strategic action plan, called 'Plans for Change'. This broad ranging review examined the organisation's mission, its strategic aims, the priorities for development from 1993 to 1997, and the ways in which working practices would need to change in support of the programme. The changes to working practices were enveloped within the term 'New Directions' and included moves from:

- long to short response times
- complexity to simplicity
- provider-led to customer-centred provision
- an expenditure to an income culture
- centralism to subsidiarity
- quality control to quality assurance.

The family tree of New Directions starts with the University's policy document 'Plans for Change' and the Training and Development Unit's own policy document. This emphasises development for all staff, and that development activity should be individually rooted. The Staff Committee Action Plan which incorporates this is communicated to all staff. Plans for Change recognised the need for staff involvement to make change happen and acknowledged the need for a mechanism to support this. The Pro-Vice Chancellor, Strategy wanted to involve and consult with staff about the strategic plan and enlisted the help of the Training and Development unit in Personnel to make this a reality. From this desire, the New Directions workshops were created. Over time the 'New Directions' programme evolved in response to the issues raised and as members of staff formed an informal ginger group, putting some energy and enthusiasm into the organisation, helping it become more radical and responsive.

The development context

The Open University approach to development was different from our other case studies, being aimed at organisational development rather more directly than the other organisations. Their primary focus had been on individual development from which organisational development might flow. This focus gave the initiatives at the University a rather different flavour.

The New Directions programme itself was a series of workshops originally intended to encourage ownership and involvement in the University's strategic plan by all staff. Originally people were contacted from the phone book to form a diagonal slice through the organisation and from here the workshops took off. As the programme progressed, it emerged that the way to unlock people's creativity, to get them to speak openly and equally at all levels of the organisation was through the use of unusual techniques, an informal atmosphere and creative facilitation. Individuals were encouraged to work with people they do not know, to have fun, to loosen up, to explore the use of metaphors. It began as a way to involve staff but became something much more as teams started to put on events themselves. New Directions moved on to explore main emerging themes either for the University as a whole of for individual departments. One of the key people behind New Directions embraced some of the principles of chaos theory, which encouraged a basic acceptance of letting things go where they will.

Real changes came from the programme: one issue raised was on the harmonisation of conditions, a staff attitude survey was supported, and an in-house calendar developed as a competition that explored drawing as a way of releasing creativity. There followed a series of communication workshops for administration units, highlighted as a development need by a 360 degree review process. The University believed that the concepts of the learning organisation had been influential to a degree, with New Directions seen as fitting comfortably alongside the learning organisation concept.

Apart from New Directions, there were also a number of other development events aimed at the delivery of skills and knowledge. These include an experienced manager programme using action learning. The University was moving in the direction of competencies with 360 degree feedback for needs analysis and for the appraisal of the senior team. This has since cascaded to middle managers. The general aim was to encourage the units to take responsibility for development and, with the help of the Training and Development Unit, the 45 units each set up their own unit plan which included a training plan. Helping units think about training for now and for the future drew the emphasis away from the existing training programme. One of the outcomes was a move away from an organisation that was resistant to change to one where there is a growing awareness of the need to change. There is also a perception that it has become more open.

Barriers include some of the individuals who helped to create the University and who are therefore very wedded to the organisation they created. Overall, the place is big and complex with procedures to match.

Sainsbury's Supermarkets Ltd

Background

Sainsbury is one of the UK's top food retailers. Until relatively recently they were comfortably the market leader but have lost market position to a rival. They characterised themselves as being somewhat complacent as an organisation up to this point, but having to reconsider their position in the light of growing competition. Traditionally, the company had not tended to view other organisations as potential learning opportunities, believing that the business probably had more to teach than to learn. The increasingly competitive environment, coupled with a business shock has changed that view. The organisation responded positively to the situation by focusing on strategy and a business planning cascade involving the key management team. This enabled them to regain focus and they engaged in a large quantity of management learning and a process of fully involving staff in the business strategy.

The organisation now takes an active interest in organisational learning. They are on the steering group of the National Campaign for Learning, working to create an appetite for learning and development and an appreciation of its everyday occurrence. The MBA programme was just one of a number of development events that were designed to create a far more positive learning culture that the organisation believed was needed to ensure robust recovery.

The development context

The MBA programme commenced in 1987 and complemented other management development programmes. The target group was middle managers with potential. The course itself and the integral involvement of City University Business School (CUBS) arose from a partnership of employers who were all looking for an MBA that would be part time, practical and aimed at improving business. The MBA covers three areas: skill, knowledge and business development. Participants are allocated to learning sets which are balanced in terms of learning styles. Each individual is allocated an educator from the university to provide academic support, and an internal coach whose role is to broker the internal environment within the organisation. During the course individuals elect from a number of taught modules and complete three projects which are assessed by the coach, the educator and the university. The MBA is unique in its emphasis on personal development and understanding self and impact.

Other than the CUBS' MBA, Sainsbury also offers the Open University MBA which has proved to be a more practical option for stores staff based long distances from London. There is also a Masters in Sales and Marketing, and lively stores-based learning for stores staff.

This learning centres on understanding the needs of the customer and how stores staff can make a difference.

3 Learning Processes

We begin our discussion of the story that emerged from our case studies by looking at the understanding amongst those we interviewed of the concept of learning. Learning is a subtle concept that encompasses a range of activities and outcomes. Given that much of our discussion with individuals was centred on their learning experience it seemed important to understand better their concept of the term. We had some thoughts that learning might be construed differently on the basis of managers' learning experience.

3.1 What is learning?

We expected that those managers that had been through an experiential learning process might be more sophisticated in their views of how they construed learning than those who had primarily experienced traditional knowledge based courses. In fact there was little support for this view. Managers' concepts of learning seemed broadly to fall within four main categories:

- learning seen as a process
- learning as an acquisition
- learning as embodying change
- learning as a growth in understanding.

3.1.1 Learning as process

Those that saw learning as a process spoke of learning as being something that happened as a outcome of another activity. Process comments might describe learning as resulting from the way managers performed their job and the change in this, or as resulting from attending training courses or from watching and observing others. Process comments were the most frequently made comment from all interviewees.

> 'It's a process — not of being told something but of watching and absorbing — being able to put that information in a way that is useful. Learning is about looking and being aware.'
>
> *The Open University*

> 'Looking for the nice theoretical description, using experience to improve effectiveness.'
>
> *The Post Office*

3.1.2 Learning as acquisition

Some managers referred to learning as the acquisition of techniques, skills, knowledge and theory. The most common belief was that learning was about acquiring knowledge, the most common individual response overall.

> 'Acquiring knowledge that can be used, or expanding existing knowledge.'
>
> *Marks and Spencer*

> 'Acquiring knowledge and new or refined ways of doing things.'
>
> *Marks and Spencer*

> 'Learning is anything that changes the way I behave and increases my stock of knowledge.'
>
> *The Post Office*

3.1.3 Learning as change

This was actually the most infrequent category of response along with learning as understanding. This category includes seeing learning as growing and adapting; of thinking more widely; of personal progress; of becoming a brighter better person; of a change in attitude. Interestingly, only one comment was made in this category by a manager in Marks and Spencer. This was the opposite of what we might have expected given the emphasis of the Marks and Spencer programme on personal change.

> 'Learning makes you more aware, conscious of the differences, implicit opportunities, interactions and learning, its about

growing, adapting and moving, not stagnating. You take what you can and apply it elsewhere.'

The Open University

'In a work context, it's a mix of drawing on experiences, techniques and skills, constantly adapting and updating the way you do your job, adding things to the armoury.'

The Post Office

'Learning that there is more than one way to do things — changing attitudes.'

Marks and Spencer

3.1.4 Learning as understanding

Comments included learning as understanding how others think and feel and understanding the differences between individuals. Interestingly, the only people who spoke of learning as also about understanding self were the Sainsbury MBA students, which reflects the strong emphasis of their MBA programme on self-development and understanding.

'It's personal understanding, being able to better myself and my position, come out a brighter, better person with better understanding of the world and how others think and feel.'

The Open University

3.1.5 Mixed models

Some of the comments could be seen to be a mix of categories:

'It's understanding a new way of doing things — a process or a method, and then being able to do something as a result of this understanding.'

Sainsbury's Supermarkets Ltd

3.2 How do managers learn?

Managers learn through a wide variety of experiences and opportunities. When asked for their perceptions of how they had learnt they often mention formal development experiences but they also mention other less formal experiences, the impact of others, job experiences, reflection *etc.*

3.2.1 Formal Programmes

Formal programmes are those events that take place off-the-job and are deliberately designed to provide a learning opportunity:

- development events/formal training
- workshops
- management education programmes
- formal study
- lectures.

> 'You learn skills through training and development and then practice those skills. Most organisations send individuals away to learn the theory and practice when they return. But there is a time lag and they forget.'
>
> *The Post Office*

Not surprisingly, they were frequently mentioned by those we spoke to, although their impact could be very variable. Such events could vary enormously in terms of their length, their design, their objectives and the learning they intend to deliver.

3.2.2 From the job

Learning from the job encompasses the learning opportunities that are provided by the work environment. These can include day to day opportunities within the job and more unusual new job or new role experiences. 'From the job' learning can be formal; in that it is a deliberate attempt to provide development opportunities, or informal *ie* the development opportunities are opportunistic. There was also variety in terms of the degree to which the individual was responsible for realising the learning opportunity and the degree to which the organisation helped create the right learning environment:

- cross functional and intra-organisational moves
- cross-organisational moves
- secondments
- project working

- extending/stretching oneself
- incidental learning
- deputising.

> 'I have a very clear view, hence job moves — these aren't just accidental but part of my IDP (Individual Development Plan).'
>
> The Post Office

3.2.3 From others

Learning from others included any development whose primary focus was on another person who helped the individual manager do things differently. As such it might overlap with other categories, *ie* there might be an element of formal learning or learning from the job, but the key to the learning taking place was the presence of some significant other:

- from others — mentors/coaches/role models
- feedback from others
- networking.

> 'I learnt a lot from people around me and the market in which I operate.'
>
> Sainsbury's Supermarkets Ltd

For some there was the presence of a learning coach, either formally acting as a mentor and creating and helping the individual to reflect on learning experiences, or in the shape of some deeply charismatic and able person who through their own capability became a role model. Such role models were mentioned by five of our managers and seemed to be the result of the good fortune to be working for someone who was inspirational in their ability to deal with others. Where such individuals had been encountered they occupied a central role in the development of a manager, and were of unusual influence. Their passing was frequently missed and their ability to change managers for the better, a much appreciated skill.

> 'When I worked for the chairman he would never go in with his boots and give someone a good kicking, it simply was not necessary. Once, someone had written a strong letter which was inaccurate and almost slanderous and someone responded with a superb letter that almost smouldered on the table and I was very

impressed. However when I showed it to X he said "I can't send this, how can I sign this? All you do is make an enemy for no good reason".'

The Post Office

'The only thing that makes any lasting change is role modelling, ie do things the same as your current boss.'

Marks and Spencer

These 'influential others' could exert their influence by pulling people towards them, which was the effect of those who acted as relatively unaware role models, or for some, by pushing the learner much more pro-actively in the direction they felt they should go.

'X facilitates people digging into themselves, for this reason it won't appeal to everyone, it could be quite threatening to some.'

Sainsbury's Supermarkets Ltd

'X's role is to push you outside of your comfort zone. A lot of what he says is crap, some of it is very good, maybe he has to be so extreme to pull people even part of the way. He is man on a mission, a visionary with semi-religious zeal. I tend to reject that approach, I have to handle the extremes. But the business is moving towards his views; the learning organisation; cross-functionalisation; cross-culture. If X's influence makes this difference then it is good.'

Sainsbury's Supermarkets Ltd

For most of our managers there had not been a mentor figure of this stature, and although learning from others was important, this was not from the perspective of quite deliberately engineered support.

3.2.4 Reflection

Learning from reflection demonstrated a more conscious appreciation of the learning experience. For some managers there was articulation of not merely the learning experience but also a deliberate internal attention to it and an integration of that experience into themselves:

- learning through doing — making mistakes
- reflection.

These reflective processes were helped by the presence of feed-back opportunities which some of our managers mentioned quite deliberately. All of our managers that mentioned feedback as a way of learning were from Marks and Spencer where feedback forms a vital part of the management development programmes. Marks and Spencer managers would also frequently mention learning through support from others, setting personal learning contracts, through disclosure, questioning self and reflection. Some of our Post Office managers also mentioned support; these were managers who had been through one of the Personal Development Workshops where they were asked to consider their career with peer support and set personal learning goals. A number of managers mentioned learning from mistakes, using experimentation and observation as learning opportunities. These were split between The Post Office, Marks and Spencer and the Open University which had deliberately encouraged people to learn from mistakes via a workshop as part of the New Directions programme:

> 'It gave me the opportunity to stand back and think how to capitalise on mistakes, it focused my thinking and now I have a more positive attitude, I encourage others to take on more risk-taking behaviours.'
>
> The Open University

Many managers from all organisations mentioned new job experiences, a new role, a new environment, having to deal with much more senior people *etc.*

When we look at the ways our managers said they had learnt, we can see that they responded in ways that were conditioned by their learning experiences. Those that had undergone a predominately knowledge-based course were more likely to consider they learnt through the acquisition of knowledge: this included managers from all our case study organisations. Those that had participated in action learning sets were much more likely to mention feedback and support.

There is an interesting difference between the impact of experience on the perception of managers of *how* they learn, compared with the apparent lack of influence on their under-standing of *what learning is*. Their experience has changed their understanding of how they as individuals learn, but does not appear to have changed their more philosophical concepts of learning *per se*.

3.3 Making learning conscious

We can conclude that managers use a variety of life experiences from which to learn, some of which are intentional, whilst others are the product of chance and good fortune. Interestingly, managers rarely saw themselves as intentional learners and would often comment that they did not learn well or consciously from what was going on around them. Those that had learned quite deliberately through observation and reflection were in the minority. Most, it seemed, fell over major learning experiences that they remembered and learnt from, precisely because they were so unavoidable. Presumably there were many other less obvious potential experiences that they passed by unaware. This puts in context the learning that managers reported as coming from work based experience. It was frequently mentioned and yet when coupled with a relatively unaware learning style it can be seen that work based learning is likely to be *ad hoc* and erratic at best.

> *'I keep a checklist of experiences called the experience monitor. I document what I learnt about certain experiences, and by committing it to writing it kind of consolidates the learning.'*
>
> The Post Office

> *'Conscious learning needs ... skills of perception and awareness, its something I've always done, in fact I've been criticised in the past for not always throwing in, I often sit back and wait and see how the land lies ...'*
>
> Marks and Spencer

What did appear as a recurring theme was the importance of other people in the learning process who could help the transition from experience to learning. It seems that others do this through holding a mirror to the learner so that they can see much more clearly the impact of what they do, or by showing them a better way of behaving. These learning helpers can be formally assigned to this role, as in those that act as coach or mentor, or those peers who participate in action learning sets. Alternatively, they can play their role completely informally. In this case they may do so unknowingly; being observed and modelled as they go about their job; or more directly by explaining why they do what they do to a learner who is sufficiently impressed by them to copy them.

3.4 Fitness for purpose

The outcomes from learning can be one of several things and different learning processes appear to be better at producing certain outcomes than others. Learning processes include training, education and personal development. Learning outcomes include change in skills, knowledge, understanding and insight.

Learning processes vary along a continuum from Training through Education to Development. Training tends to be quite specific and task focused. It implies preparing someone through demonstration and practice to be able to perform a key skill better than they could before. Of course, the term has been used more widely in organisational contexts to refer to almost any kind of learning activity. Education generally refers to a more broad based learning process with a stronger emphasis on the acquisition of knowledge and the ability to integrate that knowledge into underlying theories and concepts. Development is a more holistic concept and individuals use the term to describe some kind of personal journey, a progression towards a better person.

> 'The BMP is really a management education programme. Inasmuch as you can distinguish between education and training this one was education. The best way of telling them apart is to think of it as if you had children and they came home from school and told you that they have had sex training, then you'd worry and hope they meant sex education.'
>
> The Post Office

From our interviewees, it would seem most acquire knowledge best through formal education and training or through on-the-job learning. Skills are acquired most readily through specific on-the-job experiences and formal training in about equal measure. Acquiring understanding is a different matter and implies a deeper learning than that required for assimilating facts. It implies the mapping of new knowledge onto mental models so that it may be more accessible to the learner, or may in fact change the mental models of the learner so that their comprehension is expanded. Understanding is acquired in many ways but least well by a formal taught course. Changing mental models requires a deeper insight, a more radical learning experience than that available from a predominately fact-based course. Insight might be described as the 'ah-hah' of learning, seeing not just how something works but also why it works that way.

We saw several examples of increased understanding. There were the experiences of many who had taken part in the Open University's New Directions who had found a greater appreciation of the University's structure, the work of colleagues in different parts of the organisation, the workings of the committee system, and an appreciation of how others viewed their own department. Because of the fragmented structure of the organisation and its great complexity, and also the relatively junior position of many of those we interviewed, this insight was a unique experience and one they found very useful. It was the ability to meet others from these units and work with them towards a common aim that made the experience especially meaningful. The study also had the opportunity to see a very similar growth of understanding amongst much more senior managers in Marks and Spencer's Senior Management Consortium Programme. In this programme, senior executives were given a similar insight into the workings of those from other organisations. The executives we spoke to saw this experience as particularly meaningful. They saw their horizons lifted in a similar way to the University people who had experienced life outside their own units. For the Marks and Spencer executives, the consortium programme gave them sufficient depth of experience of the other organisations that had taken part to begin to understand not only the way these organisations looked at functions such as marketing, but also the differences of organisational culture. This gave them the ability to see their own organisation in a much wider context and to question the appropriateness of culture and the way things were done.

4 What is Learnt

We asked our managers what they thought they had learnt from the learning experiences that they were describing, and although their responses were obviously many and varied and covered an extraordinary array of human endeavour, these learning outputs divided into five main categories:

4.1 Technical knowledge

Perhaps the most obvious learning impact for individuals is the acquiring of knowledge or skill that they did not possess prior

Table 4.1 Five categories of learning

What is learned — overall category	Examples given
1. Knowledge	technical skills the technical skills of outsourcing
2. Management skills	people management strategic thinking management skills
3. Greater understanding of the organisation	seeing the bigger picture business organisation
4. Better understanding of impact on others	giving space to subordinates understanding of own impact on others and how to deal with it
5. Better understanding of self	personal skills/self skills understanding of own thought processes self-awareness/assessment

Source: IES

The Institute for Employment Studies

to the learning event, whether that be a formal course or an informal on-the-job learning event. This is what most people automatically think of when they are asked about what they had learnt.

> 'When I think back to the courses that I have really enjoyed, they have been those with a technical element.'
>
> *Marks and Spencer*

Some of this knowledge or skill acquisition was of a formal kind and correlated perfectly with the learning objectives of the course. For example, individuals acquired computing skills from a computing course and others acquired negotiating skills from a negotiating and influencing course.

> 'I attended a disciplinary workshop that went through the procedures and how to apply it. That was very beneficial as it came at a time when I hadn't had much experience of disciplinaries.'
>
> *Marks and Spencer*

The emphasis of The Post Office Business Management Programme (BMP), had been on strategic thinking, and many felt that this had been very helpful to them in developing their strategic thinking skills. These individuals had confirmed the course as a success as they had gained from the course exactly what it had intended to deliver. But also within this knowledge and skills category of learning output, there were those who had acquired some 'emergent learning' (Megginson, 1994). This was learning that had emerged from the learning event in some unexpected way, as it was not part of the learning objectives for the event. An example is from the University where one individual had taken the style of the event and had used it to facilitate an event of her own. In this way she had acquired facilitation skills from the facilitators themselves in direct modelling.

> 'I found the process fascinating and have actually used it myself. I was asked to do a session at a conference . . . employed the process and achieved a very interesting result and feedback.'
>
> *The Open University*

4.2 Management skills

Another cluster of comments was of learning how to manage better. Nearly two-thirds of comments in this category came from our Marks and Spencer's managers. They would speak of understanding individuals and their needs better, of accepting people as bringing to work lots of other issues from other parts of their lives. For the University people, the New Directions programme gave them a unique ability to work with others at very different grades from very different parts of the university. This prompted the comment from some of the more junior people that we interviewed, that they had learned how to work with different people in pursuing an end. For other managers the trigger was the receipt of feedback from subordinates on their management style.

'The thing I took away from it . . . is that I have been too ready in the past to let subordinates get on by themselves — the feedback showed that they would appreciate it if I gave more guidance.'

Government Department

4.3 The organisation

The Open University and Marks and Spencer were the only organisations where interviewees spontaneously mentioned that they had learned about their organisation.

In the Open University this was a two way learning, both of how others viewed them and their department, *ie* understanding better how they were perceived by colleagues, and also of learning how the parts of the university fitted together. It was clear that the University was a very complex organisation where the constituent parts had considerable autonomy and where there was little movement between them. As many of the people we interviewed were not managers, and frequently relatively low in the organisational hierarchy, this understanding helped them get to grips with an organisation that they had never really comprehended. Whether this would also be true for more senior people is less likely and indeed we had no such similar comments from the more senior people we interviewed.

'I learnt an awful lot more about the way people perceive how others operate within the organisation.'

The Open University

I learnt a lot about the way the committee system of the university works . . . it has a structure which I find incredibly difficult sometimes to understand.'

The Open University

Through the executive consortium programme, the Marks and Spencer managers had also acquired a greater understanding of other organisations and their cultures and approaches to work and organisational life. This learning had gone deep and enabled these executives to question much more openly the appropriateness of the Marks and Spencer way of doing things. This wasn't a brief dip in to another organisation, as might be gained through a benchmarking exercise, but was an in-depth view offering much greater insight into a number of organisations with great openness and honesty.

4.4 Impact on others

Another distinctive category was related to a deeper understanding about self, but with a clearer focus on how individual style affects other people. This was an inner understanding that had turned out again to look at how the individual's way of being, in turn affected those around them. Again these insights were predominately from the Sainsbury's and Marks and Spencer managers but not exclusively. Five of our Marks and Spencer interviewees mentioned that they had learned how they impacted on other people, peers and subordinates. Two other Marks and Spencer managers spoke of learning to network better and of being more collaborative in their working style. Another manager spoke of a difficult staff management experience which taught him not to attempt to change things too radically in one go, if you want to bring people with you. In this circumstance the change attempt had generated considerable and vocal staff opposition. One of our Post Office interviewees spoke of learning to capture the hearts and minds of people in any change attempt, and another of learning how they tended to deal with people and how to handle people better on a one-to-one basis better.

'I am more considerate more able to see the others' point of view, far less argumentative, much more constructive and with far greater tolerance levels.'

Sainsbury's Supermarkets Ltd

Reflecting the University approach of bringing individuals together, and sharing experiences and views of the university and University life, one of our University interviewees spoke about realising that they had learned not to assume that everyone shared their understanding, and that there was ignorance in some areas of what others took for granted.

4.5 Learning of self

We had numerous examples of learning about self, all from the Marks and Spencer and Sainsbury's managers. In both organisations, managers had been through development programmes that had provided considerable feedback on personal style and effectiveness, and where a strong emphasis of the programme had been on learning about individual strengths and weaknesses. For example, one manager commented that he had learned how to deal with feedback and accept it in a constructive way. Another, that they had considered where they were on their career path and to reflect on what they now wanted from their remaining career in the light of work/life balance. Another mentioned that they had realised they tended to evaluate people rather quickly and that these first impressions could be wrong. Consequently they were trying to suspend judgement on others until they had more information. Two other Marks and Spencer managers spoke of learning to be clearer about their personal style and in what ways they would like to change it to make themselves more effective. For one of these, it was to adopt a more risk-taking style in recognition of their more typical guarded approach to things. This meant that they were slow to react as they tried to gather as much available data as possible before risking a response. Another acknowledged the need to project themselves more if they were to make an impression on other managers.

> '... toughening and sharpening my act with a view to progressing. I've done a lot of work on self-projection and promotion — making opportunities to be seen, in the right places, right committees.'
>
> Marks and Spencer

'I tend to become more frustrated with people and with the job. I want to have the opportunity to change things. I no longer blame things on managers but take the initiative to make the difference. I'm more confident in every way; part of that comes from understanding myself.'

Sainsbury's Supermarkets Ltd

4.6 Negative responses

Not everyone felt positive about their learning experiences, some had not learned things that they might have expected to have learnt. Typical of this latter group were comments from a manager at Marks and Spencer that their management development programme had not increased their knowledge and from the Open University that they had not learned anything about themselves. It is clear that these comments show an expectation/ outcome mismatch between the predominant learning style of the event and the expectations that individuals had about learning. To understand this better we need to return to our interviewees' understanding of what learning was, with knowledge and skills featuring high on the list. We might expect therefore that a learning experience that is not designed to give knowledge-based outputs will not match the expectations of some of the learners.

'I hoped I would learn but we only just scratched the surface. New Directions tries to be very democratic and allow everyone their say, some individuals can get on their soapbox.'

The Open University

This mismatch was clearly found where the learning event was unusually focused on the acquisition of self-understanding, where the experiences of most individuals leaves them least prepared for this kind of learning experience. In Marks and Spencer these expectations were to some extent reduced by the interactions between those that had previously attended the course and those that were about to attend. Mostly, there were quite accurate perceptions of the unusual nature of the event.

'I had heard so many stories, peoples' lives had been transformed, they dealt with issues they hadn't dealt with before, people were being stripped down and built up again ... gave more than I got, but I wasn't expecting to get a lot.'

Marks and Spencer

The Sainsbury's programme caught many more people unawares because of the much smaller population of individuals that had attended. This made internal intelligence more difficult to get hold of and many came to the course with expectations of an MBA with the focus on knowledge, and found instead a heavy focus on self-development. Most found this refreshing but for some the mismatch was such that they found the approach very hard to accept or engage with.

> 'The MBA is based on knowledge, self and skills. It wants you to take yourself to bits and put back together again — some don't want to know themselves too well, they just want to get on with it. I felt uncomfortable with the way it was forced upon you — if you're being pushed to find what isn't there you're left feeling very hollow . . . the self-development thing hasn't done anything for me.'
>
> Sainsbury's Supermarkets Ltd

Probably the most negative comments that we received were from the Government Department participants who had completed a senior management development centre using 360 degree feedback and a variety of psychometric tests. The centre was intended to be the beginning of a development programme, but when we visited, the follow-up development events had not occurred (in part because of the relatively poor feedback from those that had attended). The managers we interviewed commented that they did not learn anything they did not know already, and they were not stimulated to do better things. Some found the subordinate and peer assessment intrusive, whereas others felt that this had not been a problem and confirmed their own view about themselves. The event did not seem to generate the team spirit that we have seen in other such events. Peer support groups were not formed. The event was not residential and therefore people did not mix after the work of the day — and indeed would not even lunch together. It seemed that individuals remained guarded rather than entering into the spirit of the occasion.

> 'The event met my expectations but these were low; the assessment from my peers and my manager never arrived. I didn't learn a lot, it was more corroborating what I knew already. The event didn't stir or stimulate me to greater or better things, it was comforting that my staff management was as expected — I was no worse than others on the course.'
>
> Government Department

'Didn't get as much out of it as I thought I might. I'm not aware of any particular area for change. Did get some knowledge that I can't apply yet. A lot of the course was designed for line managers, and as I'm not one it is difficult to apply what I learned — there were no surprises.'

Government Department

'It has a short term effect . . . I thought about what I was doing for a week or so and then drifted back.'

Government Department

'My impression is fairly negative; too many areas were covered, it was a question of snatching at issues, just touching the surface.'

Government Department

One of our Open University respondents also spoke negatively of their experiences of becoming involved in the New Directions workshops, another mentioned that they had never learnt anything worthwhile on courses and all their valuable learning had been through on-the-job experiences. This experience was echoed by one of our Post Office managers who stated that courses change knowledge but not behaviour or attitudes.

4.7 The views of others

We expected an important part of this study to be the collection of a 360 degree view on individuals who had been through the programmes that we were focusing on. In practice this proved to be very difficult to collect. One of the key issues was the movement of individuals within the organisations we studied. In reality there was very little stability in the reporting relationships which would have made it possible for us to explore the development of individuals from the perspective of others. The limited views that we did collect, confirmed the views of individuals: high impact programmes for individuals tended to be those where subordinates and line managers also noticed a difference. Those events that individuals tended to be negative about were also those that others confirmed as having little impact.

We explicitly gathered subordinate and/or line manager views within Sainsbury's, the Government Department, the Open University and The Post Office. In Marks and Spencer, the programmes we looked at were so wide ranging within the organisation that there were very few people who had not been on a similar developmental event themselves. Staff movements thereby made it impossible for the organisation to find us line managers and subordinates who had been involved with the participants both before and after the development event. A significant number of our Marks and Spencer participants were also very senior managers for whom a line manager perspective could only have been supplied by board members.

Within the Government Department the views of those around the individuals who attended the course were very mixed and reflected the fairly neutral to negative responses that we had collected from the individuals themselves. Line managers generally seemed to have been disappointed that the event did not produce the change that they wished for or anticipated.

> 'The course didn't give guidance as to where to now, if the problems are with an individual's character, no training is going to change that.'

> 'There wasn't enough detail, I hoped it would look at overcoming internal barriers.'

Subordinates voiced a similar if rather more bluntly put view:

> 'In terms of a structured learning programme, it was complete crap.'

> 'I asked how the course had gone and got a very negative response.'

Not all were as negative as this, some spoke of their manager becoming more organised, more aware of their role as a manager and what this entails, but the majority view was that there had been no visible difference.

In Sainsbury's, the difficulties of line manager and subordinate continuity were exacerbated by the MBA population being more mobile than others within the organisation. This group were frequently used as project workers and therefore could move many times within the period of the MBA. This, coupled with the extended length of the programme, meant the line manager relationship was not the best one from which to view individual development. Luckily we were able to talk to a number of coaches which are assigned to MBA students throughout the period of their study. These coaches generally had quite positive views of the development of individuals on the MBA, seeing their progress primarily in personal developmental terms.

> '*The personal development slant is the most valuable part of the course, you also meet academics and others. It is a very widening experience. Those that go through it tend to get on. During the programme individuals tend to mature, they start with very naive views, the pressure is an experience in itself, they learn to cope with the pressure and manage it.*'

> '*Participants find out about their own feelings through X's influence. It encourages people not to be afraid of what they find inside, it can be a force for great good, it can be very creative. I believe personal change is more likely as a result of the MBA and happens more quickly.*'

> '*I'm unsure if there is much transfer to the organisation; people do however manage in a different way, their attitudes to people change. It does cause ripples.*'

The Open University was also able to provide the opportunity to us to speak to both subordinates and line managers of those that had attended workshops. The impact of the New Directions programme was, however, much more organisationally focused than individually focused, and therefore our debate here was on the impact of the programme on the University rather than on the individual participants. Subordinates were generally more negative about the impact of New Directions than were the line managers of those that had participated. Subordinates were not generally aware of what had happened as a result of the workshops, and felt that some initiatives had failed through lack of support. There was a general view that the initiative had less impact now than it once did. One individual who had been quite closely involved with the New Directions team was more aware than the others we spoke to of the initiatives that had evolved from New Directions, such as the staff survey and the harmonisation of terms and conditions. Line managers were generally better informed, but even here some did not appreciate that the staff survey was as a result of a 'New Directions' workshop. There was a much more positive sense of the impact on the organisation and the way in which the approach had become embedded and therefore less visibly part of 'New Directions'.

Overall, where we were able to collect the views of others in a reporting relationship to our event participants, they confirmed the overall impression we had collected from the participants themselves.

4.8 Overview

It has to be remembered that this was predominately a management population, and hence the emphasis was on soft skills. Nevertheless, this emphasis is interesting as these have proved traditionally to be amongst the most difficult to develop and where organisations have placed considerable resources. These people skills are believed to be the key to future business success (Mitrani *et al*, 1992; Kettley and Strebler 1997). New ways of working have meant that managers are expected to encourage greater autonomy in their workforce than previously. They are expected to facilitate individuals managing their own learning and taking control of their own development and careers. This means abandoning an authoritarian management style for one that engages with the job holder much more. For individuals to use line managers as a resource in their own development, requires a relationship of trust and openness where there is genuine dialogue between the people involved. And yet organisations find that they have too many managers who cannot get close to their employees, who do not communicate effectively and who cannot coach employees to better performance. Formal, conscious development, that can improve these key capabilities should be in great demand, and we have seen that such development is possible if the development event is carefully chosen and well implemented.

We have seen that managers learn in many different ways from many different experiences, and they learn many different things from these experiences. The most interesting thing, however, is that these are not independent. What managers learn is directly related to how they learn.

- Managers learn about themselves through feedback, challenge and support.
- They learn about others by understanding themselves better and by being given the opportunity to give feedback to, and to help, others.

The Institute for Employment Studies

- Managers understand their own organisations and others better by being given detailed access to the differences in a way that is open and sharing and based on mutual learning.
- Managers learn new knowledge through formal courses, distance learning, and access to more knowledgeable people.
- They learn skills through courses that involve a degree of practising, or through on-the-job experience, or through the mentoring or coaching of another.

There is no one best way to learn, just as there is no one best thing to learn. But there is a need to ensure that the way individuals learn is suited to the learning purpose. If organisations want their managers to become more skilled at handling others, more able to use their own resources in a different way, stronger and better able to deal with feedback and use it to grow, then a traditional knowledge-based course will not deliver this objective.

5 Impact of Learning on Individuals

5.1 High impact learning events

We asked managers if they could recall any learning events that had particular impact on them. We were interested to see how managers viewed the learning they had undertaken to see if anything particularly stood out amongst all the learning they believed they had experienced. What did they think had made the most difference to them, and were there any commonalties between these high impact learning events? The events that

Table 5.1 High impact learning events

Type of event	Specific mentions
Formal programme	• CUBS/University MBA (Sainsbury's Supermarkets Ltd)
	• BMP programme (The Post Office)
	• Counselling course (Marks and Spencer)
	• Development workshops (Marks and Spencer)
	• MDP (The Post Office)
	• Benchmarking project (Marks and Spencer)
From others	• Line manager (Marks and Spencer, The Post Office)
Reflection	• Self help learning groups (Marks and Spencer)
Life events	• Getting married (Marks and Spencer)
	• Going to Hong Kong (Marks and Spencer)
	• Daughter being hurt (Marks and Spencer)

Source: IES 1998

managers mentioned are shown in Table 5.1.

In the vast majority of cases the events mentioned were of the kind that took people outside of themselves, that shocked them in some way. In some cases these shocks were entirely personal, such as one manager who told us of a time when his child was badly injured in an accident. Time spent away from work waiting to see if the child would recover made him realise the balance in his life was wrong and needed to be restored. Even when his child was well again he maintained a better balance between work and home. Another manager spoke of the shock of getting married and moving to another country with a very different culture. He had to adapt very quickly to the needs and expectations of others which were very different to his own. He found out the hard way that people have different interpretations of the same event and relationships can only be successful if these differences are treated sensitively.

Other shock events were centred on a formal development event that helped the manager think in a different way or behave quite differently. The strategic focus of The Post Office business management programme helped several managers think more strategically, which worked well in terms of their senior position and career status. Within Marks and Spencer and Sainsbury's, the shocks tended to be around seeing self differently and becoming more aware of self, how others perceived them, their strengths and weaknesses — digging into themselves in a way they had never done before, and receiving feedback of unique and startling honesty. People emerged from this experience stronger and with greater self-confidence. Some expressed it as a result of finally knowing all there is to know, nothing can hurt you any more, you learn to manage feedback because you have had so much and survived. If anything, managers on these programmes not only learned to handle feedback but to seek it out and create the opportunities for it.

5.2 The outcomes of learning

It is one thing to have learned something, but it can only be of value to others within the organisation (and indeed to the organisation itself) if this learning is applied in some way. Understanding finance better will only be of use if the job allows the application of that knowledge. Understanding the negative aspects of one's impact on others will only help if this learning is used to change behaviour. It is not enough to ask what has been learned; the key question for the impact of learning on the organisation is what the effect of that learning has been.

Once again we were struck by how much the impact of learning was dependent on the style of the learning event.

5.2.1 Cognitive style

The Sainsbury's MBA managers were much more likely to mention changes in cognitive style than the other organisations. These changes clustered into:

- strategic overview
- thinking style
- action orientation
- reflection.

Strategic overview

This cluster relates to the individual's ability to step back from the immediate issue and place it in a wider context. A broader business view was often mentioned by participants and also by coaches and HR specialists. This ability to be more strategic and place issues in context, seems to be actively encouraged during the course and is one of the role types that students are exposed to on the MBA. Around this same theme, others spoke of seeing the whole rather than the constituent parts, of making the links between issues — the systems thinking of Senge (1990). Greater political awareness was another change mentioned that fits in with this cluster. Some of those from The Post Office that had completed the BMP programme also mentioned this change in themselves.

Thinking style

The second cluster relates to the individual's changing thinking style, the way they approach problems at work and the way they think about their job and the organisation as a whole. The key themes of this cluster are clarity and creativity. It was said by participants that they were clearer about where they wanted to be and were more focused and structured in their thinking. They were also clearly more willing and able to think 'outside the box', being more creative, more radical, more willing to take risks in what they do, several describing themselves as now acting as change agents. This change was also mentioned by one of our Sainsbury's managers who had attended the Open University MBA.

> 'The programme opens up the mind, it's like looking through a misty window when the sun suddenly comes out.'
>
> *Sainsbury's Supermarkets Ltd*

Action orientation

The third cluster centres around the likelihood of doing something with regard to problems, as opposed to just thinking about possible solutions. These are natural associates and clearly complementary skills. Within this cluster are attributes of being more action orientated, taking the initiative more, being more proactive, being more assertive. For many of those that had been on the programme, these changes were expressed as different from their previous style of working. Again this ability was also mentioned by another Sainsbury's University MBA student who believed that he contributed more.

> 'I became much more proactive about my own career . . . before the MBA I would get fed up fairly quickly if no-one was doing something for me, now I do things for myself.'
>
> *Sainsbury's Supermarkets Ltd*

Reflection

The final cluster of cognitive skills is about quieter, less proactive cognitive skills, those of reflection, learning from mistakes, the skill of questioning the way a thing is done and why it should be that way. These skills were also mentioned by one of the University MBA people and by one of The Post Office people who believed that he now thought through the outcomes before acting, and a Marks and Spencer manager who stated that she had become more probing and analytical.

> 'The question I now ask myself about my job is "am I learning?" At the time I applied for the MBA I had outgrown my previous jobs, I wasn't learning any more and needed more stimulus.'
>
> *Sainsbury's Supermarkets Ltd*

'I'm more reflective, I don't know what caused it, I think more. I learnt a lot from my managers, I'm more likely to see the good and bad after the courses. I'm more probing and analytical.'

Marks and Spencer

Some of our other organisations had a predominately different emphasis tending away from cognitive style towards a more personal impact.

5.2.2 Personal style

These comments were most frequently made by our Marks and Spencer managers who spoke of becoming more open, and more honest in style. One spoke of being more willing to show the caring, sensitive side to his nature which he had kept hidden for fear that it might be thought to be a weakness. It was direct feedback that it was actually perceived to be a strength rather than a weakness that enabled him to reveal this style more often.

'Before the SMDP . . . at work I didn't develop my people side, I didn't give it any priority — when I realised how much people got from support I was unafraid to show that side at work — I realised it didn't show weakness.'

Marks and Spencer

In this same cluster was an appreciation that it was acceptable to be influenced by another and to change position on a subject; what might be seen as giving in. Another of The Post Office managers spoke of toning down their personal style as they felt they were sometimes perceived to be overly friendly — too 'smarmy'. This awareness of personal impact and the tendency to deliberately adjust style to take into account the perceptions of others was common among our senior Marks and Spencer managers and another result of the intensive feedback they had received from peers and subordinates as to the way they appeared to others.

'I've always been aware of a natural charm which can work as a advantage but which can lead you not being taken seriously. I now try to be less charming . . . I have noticed that others take my views more seriously . . . '

The Post Office

'I'm now a better listener and more sensitive to the requirements of jobs and job holders, and more aware of my and my team's impact on business performance.'

Sainsbury's Supermarkets Ltd

5.2.3 Self-awareness

Understanding of self, *ie* an intense appreciation of self and the impact individuals had on others, did not come from formal taught, knowledge based learning. Neither did it come solely from on-the-job development, or the intervention and use of role models. But we did see plenty of it, and it clearly had high impact on the learners who mentioned it. Learning about self and impact on others came from feedback from others in structured circumstances. We saw three quite separate examples:

- In Sainsbury's through the MBA programme.
- In Marks and Spencer in the executive and senior management development programme.
- In The Post Office in the Individual Development Programmes.

All these programmes created a learning environment where there was considerable individual exploration and feedback and where there was peer support.

This was another example of the use of learning helpers to enable individuals to stretch themselves, especially where the learning is difficult and contentious. To borrow from the ideas of Vygotsky (1988) it may be that learning helpers embody the social nature of learning and help the learner to leave their comfort zone into the zone of proximal development.

'Management development had a positive impact to get people to talk about the problems they're having in an environment where they can trust people to be confidential. Especially for men; men find it more difficult to talk in this way.'

Marks and Spencer

Interestingly, a similar scheme at the Government Department had very little impact on those that attended. This may have been in part because of the civil service culture, which was highly status driven and where individuals were relatively guarded. It may also have been partly because of the lack of facilitation of the journey of exploration and the failure to build peer support structures through the event. In fact many of our interviewees mentioned that the programme was non-residential and that participants tended to return to their own offices over the lunchtime and at the end of the day. Self-exploration requires a good deal of trust which can only emerge as relationships develop and are tested. If these relationships are regularly fragmented and not hothoused within the relatively short timescale of most development programmes, it is not surprising that the necessary conditions do not develop to enable people to share and explore their personal styles and approaches.

Self-image

Associated with the ability to change personal style is the accommodation of a changed self-image. These comments came most frequently from the Marks and Spencer and Sainsbury's managers, but were also mentioned by Post Office managers and University people. Most commonly this involved some kind of increase in self-confidence or self-esteem. This can be seen as a concomitant of self-awareness. Indeed more than half of those who spontaneously mentioned that an impact of their learning was increased self-awareness, also spoke of increasing confidence. Several made a direct link between the two, implying that it was the growing awareness of their own strengths and weaknesses that gave rise to a growing sense of self-acceptance and confidence. A by-product of this was the ability to value feedback more, going beyond learning to accept and use feedback but to actively seek it out and ask people for feedback in a genuinely interested way.

> 'Had much more confidence; achieved a higher degree, delivered three projects of value . . . this derives from understanding myself better.'
>
> Sainsbury's Supermarkets Ltd

> 'I gained in confidence, I found I knew a lot more than I thought I did, how areas interrelated, it opened my eyes to my own individuality.'
>
> Sainsbury's Supermarkets Ltd

> 'It has increased my confidence no end, raised my self-image and my self-awareness. It has done no end of good.'
>
> Sainsbury's Supermarkets Ltd

5.2.4 Ways of dealing with others

The other ways in which managers spoke of having changed were in their dealings with others. People spoke of being more tolerant, more sensitive, more considerate, less likely to seek to attribute blame, a better listener, more of a teamworker and of having adopted a more human, democratic management style. These comments were made by Sainsbury's, Marks and Spencer, The Post Office and one Open University manager. In contrast, another Post Office manager spoke of becoming more directive but this was in direct response to some feedback that he was not clear enough as to what he wanted done when delegating. In some circumstances our managers had become more honest. This was in response to the encouragement of a more open receptive style, the willingness to receive feedback may make it easier to give, although this may not always be a comfortable response:

> 'People say I've changed — that's not all for the best, one's innate personality doesn't change. I have become more open, I say what is in my mind — that's not all good. In early years I was very good at a public face — people were comfortable. Now I say things that kill people. I cut people's legs off. My people counsel me, people tell me not to be so nasty.'

> *Marks and Spencer*

> 'I tend to be a bit more stagy with my boss, I provide them with lots of equations and corporate plans and strategic help . . . I have learnt that ideas must have gravitas, ie there must be performance indicators to convince.'

> *Government Department*

6 Organisational Impact

6.1 Organisational change

We asked our interviewees what impact they felt their learning had had upon their organisation. In nearly all cases they found this very difficult to articulate, other than through the ways they themselves had felt they had changed. When further probed about the ways their organisations had changed over the last few years there was a much clearer articulation.

6.1.1 Egalitarian

The clearest picture of change came from Marks and Spencer. Our interviewees spoke of an organisation that had become less paternal, more commercial, less complacent, less arrogant, more willing to learn from its mistakes and also more willing to learn from others. Senior managers spoke vividly of a less competitive, more team based approach to problem solving, in marked contrast to the previous cultural style. In their consortium programme experiences, they were struck by how much more they functioned as a team compared to their senior colleagues from other organisations. No-one was confident about ascribing these organisational changes to the development programmes that we had observed and indeed this would be a gross simplification. Organisations rarely introduce initiatives in isolation and the impact of management development programmes are felt in conjunction with other initiatives that push in the same direction. Nonetheless these programmes can be seen to be consistent with the changes that we observed. The Marks and Spencer senior management programme does explicitly encourage team working, and the other management development programmes in the organisation explicitly encourage a more open egalitarian communication style.

'The SMDP and EDP had an enormous impact on the business. The timing was absolutely right. We weren't getting the most out of people. The destructive competitiveness designed to win at all costs was destructive for the business. It has changed. The informality that exists encourages open conversation on issues — much more solution seeking.'

Marks and Spencer

A greater egalitarianism is probably high on many organisations' wish lists. We have already seen that the changes impacting on organisations have tended to encourage a more democratic, participative management style. This has led to much pressure on managers, especially those in the middle of organisations that have large people management responsibilities:

'Managers from all levels have been put upon quite heavily — because in the absence of a learning organisation they are expected to cope — I have seen some who haven't and there have been casualties. Suddenly you're expected to become this much wider thinker, you know this networker, no longer an autocrat manager who says "Do this" but has to be a sensitive caring leader. And you've suddenly got to manage all this, while if you look at the core of the business, — not just ours but others, — it is still quite rigid, it hasn't really shifted and the pressure lands on the middle and senior manager.'

The Post Office

Organisations need to provide support to managers making these transitions. The middle manager is often at a key pinch-point in organisational culture when organisational learning is causing a cultural shift.

6.1.2 Flexible

The Open University interviewees also showed considerable commonality of response, describing an organisation that had become more flexible and less hierarchical, more sharing and more open with information. This too can be seen to be congruent with the style of New Directions which specifically looked at the organisation from a non-hierarchical direction. The intention of New Directions was to enhance communications and create a more open organisational culture.

'I think the University is changing a lot at the moment, some of it is attributable to New Directions, perhaps only a small amount. New Directions has been a good oil, making it go more smoothly. It was an outlet for individuals at any level to voice difficulties and uncertainties, to vocalise those in a non-threatening way.'

The Open University

6.1.3 Project based

The Sainsbury's MBA had at its heart a series of projects that students were expected to complete. These projects give a rather more direct organisational impact that the other schemes that we looked at. Most of those interviewed felt that the company was not getting as much as it should out of the MBA projects. This may reflect the project choice or the project outcome. Seven of the 23 students we interviewed made positive comments about their projects being of value. Interestingly, it tended to be the first projects that are most used rather than the later more strategic ones. This reflects the fact that the first project is centred in the individual's work area and most probably represents an area of interest to the student's line manager. These first projects tend to be simplest and most pragmatic in nature and therefore are probably the easiest to implement. Later projects which are designed to be wider in scope and to take the student out of their own area, suffer from a difficulty of buying in a project sponsor. Both students and managers mention the importance of proper project sponsorship in getting the project used. Projects which have good senior sponsors do get used, but many do not.

The MBA offers the chance to step outside and question the Sainsbury's Supermarkets Ltd management culture. Its emphasis on the inner self, on more open interpersonal styles and on self-development, are all powerfully counter-cultural. This counter-cultural element has distinct advantages in the formation of internal project teams and we saw numerous occasions where the MBA students had been picked to participate in change projects within the organisation completely separated from their existing jobs and their studies! In this way the programme was having real impact, albeit a sometimes uncomfortable one.

6.1.4 Business focus

For some organisations the change was seen to be one of business focus, the organisation had changed its perspective on the world, becoming frequently more focused on external than internal issues. Typical of these would be a focus away from a paternalism to a more commercial awareness, or from internal matters and issues to the customer and the customer's view of what the business offers.

> 'The business is massively more externally focused on business and the customer. The individual role is crucial, some drive change which is then owned by others — this is empowerment when it works.'
>
> *The Post Office*

> 'I do believe that sometimes changing things is a good idea just for the sake of keeping it alive — there is a great Woody Allen quote: "A relationship is like a shark, it has to keep moving or else it dies". An organisation is like that, it has to keep moving.'
>
> *The Post Office*

6.2 The transfer of learning

One of the key questions that we set out to answer was how does the learning of individuals transfer to the organisation. We anticipated that there might be something about the learning event or the organisations deliberate response that may have some impact on the ease with which this translation occurs.

We asked the HR practitioners within our case studies for their understanding and insight into the way their organisations acquired knowledge and understanding, but were struck by the lack of formal mechanisms to facilitate learning transfer. There were no formal systems to transfer individual learning to the organisation more widely.

So perhaps there is something in the way individuals learn that might itself influence whether and how learning is passed on through the organisation. We have seen that individuals learn through a wide variety of methods, some of which are about formal and deliberate ways to encourage individuals to learn, and others are through more informal learning experiences and insights (Table 6.1).

Table 6.1 Passing on learning

Formal programmes

- workshops
- formal study
- cross-functional and intra-organisational moves

- management education programmes
- development events/formal training

From the job

- cross-organisational moves
- project working
- incidental learning

- secondments
- extending/stretching oneself
- deputising

From others

- feedback from others
- networking

- from others — mentors/coaches/role models

Reflection

- reflection

- learning through doing — making mistakes

Source: IES 1998

In seeking to understand what facilitates transfer, one of the difficulties is that however learning takes place there is a transfer. This transfer can be from individual to individual, *eg* in learning from a trainer or facilitator, or through a mentoring relationship. Sometimes the learning is from a more diffuse cultural residence such as when learning from a new role, and sometimes it is from books or other sources. But we can see that within all these different methods of learning there is the opportunity, and indeed the necessity, for the transfer of learning between individuals or from the environment to the individual.

6.2.1 The transfer of learning to the individual

This transfer can take place through:

- the deliberate attempt of the organisation
- the formal attempts by individuals to self-manage their learning
- the actions of others acting as coaches or mentors or role models
- the experiences that the organisation offers to employees.

There are two key dimensions to learning transfer that are embodied in these examples. These are the degree of formality associated with the learning (the more formal the learning method, the more formal and explicit is the learning transfer), and the locus of control of the learning between the individual and the organisation. The interplay of these dimensions and how the common ways of learning sit between them is shown below in Figure 6.1.

Within these dimensions organisations have choices as to how they encourage learning and development:

- within individuals
- from individual learners to others
- into the wider organisation.

6.2.2 Transfer of learning from the individual to the wider organisation

Organisations can place their faith in a spectrum of approaches, from the highly formal, direct intervention at one end to the informal, 'osmosis'-like transfer at the other. For example, an organisation that wishes to use a new computer package to improve processes can:

Figure 6.1 The dimensions of learning transfer

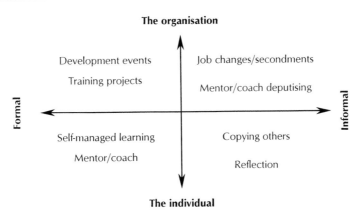

Source: IES 1998

- teach everyone how to use the package so that it becomes something that everyone can do
- set up formal mechanisms for this learning to be passed on to colleagues through a cascade process
- encourage an environment where there is an informal tendency to pass on the knowledge to others
- encourage an environment where individuals will be exposed to working with the new package and will manage their own learning
- allow the outputs from the use of the new computer package to impact on the organisation and others, and change the ways things happen.

In these options there is a move from a direct approach to learning acquisition to a more indirect approach, and from an emphasis on **inputs** to learning to one on **outputs** of learning (Figure 6.2).

6.3 The relationship between individual learning and organisational learning

Organisational learning is not easily articulated by those within organisations. Even our relatively sophisticated learners were not able to comment on organisational learning. We have seen that this may be due to the complexity of the learning process and the way it is embedded in learning method. Partly the difficulty is the essential nature of learning transfer — without transfer there would be no learning.

This is a self-evident truth, but there is much learning transfer over which the organisation has no control or influence. By tapping into the processes by which individuals learn, organisations could more clearly maximise the learning opportunities

Figure 6.2 Organisational opportunities for learning transfer

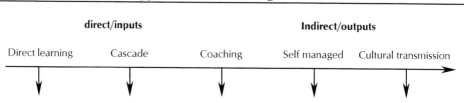

Source: IES 1998

The Institute for Employment Studies

that they create. What we have seen is that by shifting the focus from looking at organisational learning (which most could not express) to organisational change, there is considerable congruence between the learning events that the organisations were adopting and the ways in which they were changing. However, we do not know if the learning events that we examined have themselves resulted in the changes to the organisations that the participants were able to see. This may be the case, but it may also be that the learning event and organisational change process are congruent and dependent on some other, completely independent variable. This problem of 'endogeneity' has been commented on in the understanding of the contribution of training to organisational profitability, (Green, 1997) and is true of many HR processes. The chain of cause and effect in organisations is highly complex and dependent on a number of variables which may be related.

7 Other Themes

There is a well known proverb:

'You can take a horse to water but you can't make it drink'

which might fruitfully be applied to learning. Why do some of our learners refuse to drink while others take their fill; what is it about some learning events that make no-one thirsty?

The motivations for learning are very complex and trying to understand what it is that makes people want to learn has already been the subject of a considerable amount of research, (see for example Tamkin and Hillage, 1997). If we add to this what it is that makes learning successful, and in what ways it changes people, we can see that we are dealing with a complex phenomenon. Learning can be represented as a process model, whereby the entry into learning and the progression through it are dependent on certain factors (see Figure 7.1).

7.1 Inputs — The motivation of the learner

To return to our horse for a moment, it seems a logical reason for the failure to drink is that our horse is not thirsty. Similarly, perhaps some of our learners were not learning because they did not wish to, they did not have a self-recognised need. In our conversations with managers, there did seem to be some evidence that the greater the motivation of the learner the greater the likely learning. In some development programmes, individuals had attended because they had to. Their line manager had identified a weakness, or a development event was compulsory for all at a certain level or career stage. Where the individual attended unwillingly the resulting learning seemed lukewarm to say the least. But for others, even if

Figure 7.1 The learning process

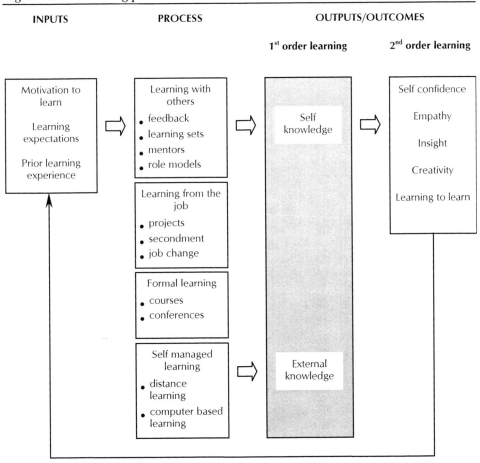

Source: IES 1998

attendance was pretty much compulsory, if the learning event was good enough and they then entered into it with some enthusiasm, they frequently got much out of it. This was most starkly put by one manager who attended a development event that involved considerable self-disclosure. The entire group was finding this very difficult and uncomfortable and so he decided that the only way to survive was to enter into it wholeheartedly. He ordered champagne and made a party out of it.

So you can lead a thirsty horse to water and it is likely to drink. If your horse isn't thirsty, it might drink anyway if you offer it champagne!

The MBA programmes were the best example of highly committed learning and where there was considerable enthusiasm for the learning. In many ways this was also the most difficult learning event that we looked at because of the length of the programme and the required time commitment. Many of our interviewees commented on the time needed and the strain this placed on their personal lives. In fact a few had either given up their studies or had become 'stuck', finding it very difficult to progress beyond a particular phase.

7.1.1 External versus internal motivation.

Closely aligned to the motivation of the learner was a theme of where the motivation for learning was coming from. This is more subtle than the degree of motivation to learn, it is more about where the motivation is centred. There are those learners who were learning for completely personal reasons. They wished to better themselves, or to learn for interest and enjoyment. For these individuals the motivation to learn was strongly internally focused. Others wanted to learn to acquire a qualification or to improve their career. Here the focus of their motivation is external (see Figure 7.2).

We might expect that external motivations are more susceptible to changing work circumstances, whereas internal motivations are likely to be more robust. There is general psychological evidence that internal motivations tend to be longer lived and lead to more lasting satisfaction (for an overview of some of the relevant literature see Tamkin and Hillage, 1997). Unfortunately we couldn't test this in our small scale study and it is confused by the fact that the reasons why people initially get involved in

Figure 7.2 Motivation to learn

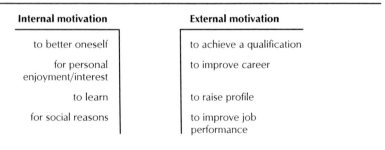

Internal motivation	External motivation
to better oneself	to achieve a qualification
for personal enjoyment/interest	to improve career
to learn	to raise profile
for social reasons	to improve job performance

Source: IES 1998

The Institute for Employment Studies

learning may be different from the reasons why they continue with learning (Tamkin and Hillage, 1997).

Why individuals want to learn is clearly important in terms of matching their needs with the likely outcome of the learning programme.

7.2 Learning processes

7.2.1 Internal vs external learning

A key difference in the learning events we have looked at, and the learning outputs as a result of these events, is where the emphasis of the learning is. Some events place learning emphasis on the outer world and the way it functions, others on the inner world of the learner and developing an understanding of this and the way it works. Thus there are two fundamental dimensions in the learning process: there is the learning that is external to the individual, and that which is internal.

The other key sub-division is between the learning of knowledge and the learning of skills. A model of these dimensions is given below which was developed by Tom Bourner of the University of Brighton. This model distinguishes those things that are part of the *outer world*; (the domains of technical and social knowledge that are available to us all, and the skills that exist in

Figure 7.3 External and internal skills and knowledge

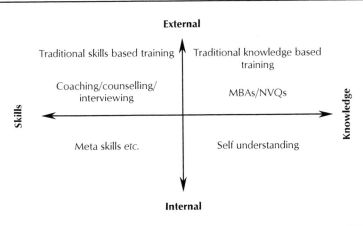

Source: Bourner, 1996

the world of work, such as computer skills, car maintenance, interviewing techniques); from the *inner world*, (the knowledge that we have of ourselves and the skills we develop to manage our unique mix of strengths and weaknesses). Functioning effectively in the outer world, especially on the boundaries of our interactions with others, is enhanced and helped by our inner understanding and the empathy that this gives us for others. To learn effectively we should appreciate our own learning styles, and we should be open to learning experiences and to challenging ourselves.

We believe the key to the learning we have seen many of our managers display, is this development of robust internal knowledge and skills.

7.2.2 Job challenge

It has been proposed that one of the key developmental components of on-the-job learning is via job challenge. Job challenge arises from a gap between the skills and abilities of the individual and those demanded by the job. Experiencing this gap motivates managers to learn what is necessary to carry out the responsibilities of the job (Baldwin and Padgett, 1993). There is some evidence that challenge also has the potential to be destructive and needs to be carefully managed if there is to be positive growth (Baldwin and Pagett, 1993). In fact research shows that when challenge becomes insurmountable, it can lead to executive derailment, and rarely provides a significant learning experience. Being able to learn from hardship experiences requires that managers are willing to examine themselves and learn from their mistakes. This is something that managers find very difficult to do, primarily because they have been successful all their lives (Argyris, 1991). It appears that the further managers advance, the more difficult they find it to receive and accept this feedback (Bartolome, 1989). Others may feel unable to provide honest feedback to executives, and the many demands and pressures faced by senior managers may inhibit them from taking the time to reflect and examine themselves. In support of this, senior executives have been found to hinder re-engineering activity by being good at supporting change but poor at changing themselves (Hout and Carter, 1993). Most of the literature around challenge concentrates on the development gap provided by new jobs or roles but we have seen that challenge can be provided by others or through development programmes.

The Soviet psychologists developed the concept of the zone of proximal development (Vygotsky, 1978), to describe that area of capability just beyond current performance into which an individual can be encouraged to develop.

> 'The key is to be taken a bit further than you think you're capable of, development has to be stretching — it's as if your shirt doesn't fit any more and you want to fill it up.'
>
> *The Post Office*

Step beyond this zone and you stretch people too far, they cannot develop but instead are overwhelmed by the experience and are likely to fail. What also appears to help in this learning from difficulty is the support of others. This takes us to the social nature of learning. This is more than learning being embedded within a cultural and social context, this is how others can act as learning helpers supporting an individual in their learning transition. These others can help the learner accept the learning challenge and to reflect and learn from it.

> 'The important thing is that the SMDP is experimental. It provides a safe environment, non-competitive. You can't get that through work — taking a risk at work is too big a risk. The SMDP encourages you to role play and take risks.'
>
> *Marks and Spencer*

Where development events fail to pose a sufficient challenge they can seem very dull and insufficiently stretching.

> 'It was a bit lower standard than I expected, I thought that we would have to work a bit harder, I wanted to be stretched and challenged.'
>
> *Government Department*

7.2.3 The importance of feedback

We have seen that feedback has occupied a central position within this research, those that have received structured feedback within a supportive and trusting environment have used this to change themselves for the better, becoming more proactive, more self-confident and more empathic in their dealings with others.

Feedback can play a positive role in enhancing self-esteem through increasing self-knowledge: see Figure 7.4.

As individuals acquire self-confidence they are more likely to seek feedback and to utilise it as a valuable tool. In this study we have seen that this is most likely to happen where individuals receive feedback initially in a supportive environment from those that they have come to trust.

> 'The SMDP has had the greatest impact out of work, it has been the most harsh feedback in my life — I was told that I wasn't a listener and that I was sensitive. It was seen as a strength. Feedback is the most important thing, if you can get honest feedback you're doing pretty well, you don't get honest feedback normally, you get political feedback.'
>
> *Marks and Spencer*

However, feedback does not always result in this virtuous circle. There are individuals who find feedback very difficult, and we have seen how in the Government Department the feedback received from the development centres and peer and subordinate review was not welcomed or well utilised. In an unsupported environment, feedback can be perceived as threatening when it tells the individual something they did not know about themselves, and are not ready to integrate into their self-knowledge. In these circumstances a vicious circle is set up. (see Figure 7.5).

It would also seem that a growing self-awareness causes individuals to deal more empathically with others. A better understanding of our own strengths and weaknesses can make us more understanding of the weaknesses of others. Similarly, understanding our own fears and motivations can enable us to arrive at a better understanding of these in others. Where this

Figure 7.4 Positive feedback

Source: IES 1998

The Institute for Employment Studies

Figure 7.5 Negative feedback

Source: IES 1998

awareness has arisen in a social setting, and where others have shared their personal development on these issues, then this understanding of others can also be gained directly.

7.2.4 The social nature of learning

It was the Russian psychologists that placed learning within a social and cultural context (*eg* Vygotsky, 1988). Their argument is that learning is not isolated from the social situation in which we find ourselves. What, and how we learn, is embedded in this cultural context and cannot be ignored.

Our society has been described as a very individualistic one (Lessem, 1994) with the emphasis on learning and working individually, and traditionally learning has occurred in a very individual passive model. It has also been said that Western society values knowledge over all other forms of knowing (Nonaka, 1995) and traditional management education has concentrated on facts and figures. These traditional models of learning and development have been challenged as the demands on managers have moved towards greater flexibility, the ability to manage change, the ability to motivate individuals, and to manage in more democratic participative ways. The old models of development did not seem to be preparing managers for this changing role, and were notably unsuccessful in changing behaviour. In this study we have seen some development programmes that have moved away from a passive, individualistic, knowledge-based learning to learning that is explorative and highly interactive, embedded in a social context and with support groups. Such learning places the emphasis on understanding self and process rather than knowledge. These development events have shown themselves to be particularly able to support management development with greater impact, that comes much closer to meeting the needs of today's managers.

'I was also really frustrated with one of my line managers who wasn't letting go, so I spoke about this on the course. My group helped me develop a clear action plan and I came back very motivated to achieve something, my group gave me lots of moral support. I was surprised how much people cared.'

Marks and Spencer

'On one person it had a great impact, you have to do a lifeplan — the six things in your life that have had a great impact. Quite a lot emerged from that he hadn't foreseen. It related closely to some of the problems he was having at work. The group pushed and supported him to work through and address things.'

Marks and Spencer

7.3 Outputs — what can you change: attitude versus behaviour?

It was said to us by a small number of individuals that we interviewed, that they thought it was not possible to change attitudes or fundamental behaviour traits through training and development. These individuals felt that the only things that courses changed were job knowledge or specific job-related skills. All of those that said this to us had been involved in knowledge-based courses. Despite this belief we did speak to many people who felt that their behaviour had changed substantially through their development experiences and in some cases the learning had gone deeper towards attitudes and behavioural traits. Such changes had been the result of intensive learning events combining feedback, support and reflection.

7.4 Putting these themes together

We suggest that the positive import of some of our development events demanded of the modern manager (which seemed particularly good at changing managerial behaviour towards them) have been closely bound up in a number of key issues:

- A foundation stone of the development of the modern manager is internal learning — the growth in knowledge about self and the skills to make the most of the unique individual.

- For this internal learning to occur, requires individuals to be pulled into new learning areas — they need to be challenged and stretched by learning opportunities.

The Institute for Employment Studies

- Learning about self is potentially a deeply uncomfortable process. It requires individuals to see and discover the unknown, and feedback plays a fundamental part in this discovery.

- Feedback is much more likely to be accepted and integrated into self-understanding if it is received in a supportive environment. The social nature of learning can provide the cultural catalyst for this. Individuals act as learning helpers, assisting learners accept and rise to the learning challenge.

- From this growth in personal understanding flows a much more empathic understanding of others, and greater awareness of impact on others.

- The result of these changes is managers who are much more likely to demonstrate fundamental changes in their approached to management.

8 Conclusions

8.1 Developing the modern manager

We have seen from this study that the development event itself is of crucial importance to the development outcome. This would not seem to be surprising news, but development processes and their applicability and relationship to outcome have received relatively little research. The point has been made by Alan Mumford in his recent review of learning processes (Mumford, 1997). He comes to the conclusion that certain kinds of learning processes are more suited to deliver certain learning outcomes. He stresses that insight is more likely to arise through action learning than through other kinds of development activity. This is a finding that this study completely endorses, although we have seen that there is a crucial role for feedback and learning to be embedded in a social context for delivering certain kinds of results for learners and their organisations.

Modern organisations demand managers that are flexible, able to adapt to change, and who possess certain key soft skills. This has been confirmed by work recently completed by IES which has emphasised the critical nature of soft skills. Among the key skill identified by this work (Kettley and Strebler, 1997) are the skills of gaining trust, of developing people, of encouraging the empowerment of others, of nurturing effective relationships, of communicating and influencing, of working with new information, concepts and strategies, of managing themselves effectively, of seeking and using feedback and of tenacity and integrity. For many organisations these skills sets require a step change in the behaviour the organisation previously rewarded.

We have seen that learning programmes with an emphasis on feedback and learning support are best placed to create reflective, empathic managers. We would also suggest that this kind of learning is unlikely to take place outside a carefully and deliberately crafted learning event. *If organisations want to develop modern managers, they need to do so consciously.*

8.2 Courses for horses

We have already pointed out that the development event needs to be chosen to match the desired development outcome. But it is also true that the development event needs to be carefully chosen in the light of the proclivities of the learner. We have seen that even those events that generally have large and lasting impact on learners, can be rejected by some. This is most likely to be the case where the event contains a strong element of self-awareness and reflection, and where the learner finds this approach uncomfortable and threatening. Unfortunately this is also the key to adopting a more open, democratic management style and therefore those that are least likely to gain from such programmes are likely to be those whose management style is unacceptable anyway. There will be situations where organisational culture does inhibit the success of certain styles of learning events. *It is important that organisations recognise that this may be so, and therefore do not engage in events that they cannot manage.* It is also true that *learner expectations and learning styles need to be taken into account if expensive learning failures are not to occur.*

8.3 Learning to learn

One of the most hoped-for outcomes from a learning event is that the learner shall emerge a more sophisticated, aware and insightful learner than when they entered. We have seen that this sophistication of the concept of learning is not easily developed, but that there is considerable difference expressed by learners as to how they learn. Those that have learned a great deal through personal feedback in the context of a supportive environment, not only continue to value feedback but actively seek it out. These are also the learners who actively ask themselves: 'Am I learning?' and look for learning opportunities in work and outside. These individuals seek challenge from a position of experiencing challenge as a positive force for change. Once again these outcomes are more likely in the context of whole-person learning programmes where the emphasis is on the individual, their reactions, their impact, rather than those where the emphasis is on knowledge. *Organisations who seek self-managing learners should look to reflective learning events.*

Appendix 1: Interview Guide

Discussion Guide for HR Managers

Strategy

Does the organisation have a strategy for development and learning?

If it does is this explicit or implicit?

What is it?

How is it communicated?

What are the objectives?

How was it arrived at? (who championed it, who created it, who was involved, does it deal with different groups of staff differently)

How is success measured/how will it be measured?

If there is no overt strategy ask what the interviewee perceives the overall belief to be? Explore the reasons for this, how inclusive it is *etc.*

Policy and Practice

What are the key approaches to development? Explore these thoroughly, how they operate, what the approach is, we need a full understanding of the kinds of initiatives, their flavour, what prompted them, what their impact has been.

Probe for

● on the job development (projects/secondments)

The Institute for Employment Studies

- coaching
- action learning
- knowledge/skills based courses
- management development
- competency based development
- use of appraisals
- pdps
- IiP

Who does this development apply to *ie* what part of the organisational population, how many (%), what grades? Are there any groups that are excluded or underrepresented? How do they know?

How is development supported *ie* manager/individual discussion, peer support, use of projects?

In what ways does the organisation encourage the application of learning in the workplace? What kind of initiatives are in place?

If appraisal is used to asses development needs and/or outcomes — Is appraisal used for other purposes *ie* pay, succession planning? Does this impact on the expression of development needs?

How does the organisation respond to mistakes, are they actively used as development opportunities?

Communication

Are there any formal systems to disseminate key information, what communication systems are in place? (probe use of IT, team meetings, upward communication?

How is communication maintained between sites, departments *etc.*

In what way is learning disseminated?(explore some examples)

What are the barriers to communication and learning across the organisation?

Barriers

What gets in the way of individual and organisational development If anything? (Probe devolution, downsizing, delayering, growing line management accountability, individual attitudes — how are these dealt with.

Impact

What has the impact of these various initiatives been?

Ask nicely how they know, what kinds of data they collect, what has worked better than others.

Development Interview

Learning

What do you understand by learning? What does it mean to you?

Looking back over the last 2-3 years what do you see as being the key things you have learned? (probe for skills, knowledge, attitudes, self understanding).

How did this learning take place? Where, what facilitated?

Either in this period or previously, is there any particular learning experience that sticks in your mind as being particularly impactful? Explore.

(Find out what was associated with this learning, what did the individual learn, how did the learning occur; formal, informal through instruction, through doing, with others. By self, degree of self control; explore concept of objective learning, *ie* that which they set out to learn versus emergent learning, *ie* that which was unexpected.)

Prompt if we are only getting formal learning examples — have you learnt anything other than on courses? Explore formal and informal learning examples thoroughly; we need to get some feel for the length of any course, its focus, how learning was facilitated, who else plays a part, the application of learning to the workplace.

What have you learned from others?

Looking back at what you have learned and the ways in which you have learned, what has had greatest impact?

Who do you consider to be important others in your learning, who provides support and help?

If they have not mentioned the learning event with which they have been identified through their organisation, probe: You have recently taken part in a learning event, what did you learn from this?

How does it compare with the other examples of learning that you have been telling me about?

Impact

In what ways do you think you have changed over the last 2-3 years? (performance at work, knowledge you bring, relationships with others, interpersonal skills, self understanding, confidence) How about outside of work?

What do you attribute this change to?

What has been the role of learning in this change?

Give me an example of how you are doing things differently?

Has the change been sustained, (if not why is this?)

What has been the response of those around you?

What has the impact of the *learning event* been? Do you feel that you have changed at all, in what ways, has this been sustained?

Others

In what ways has your learning had an impact on others?

Have you transferred your learning to others? (immediate subordinates, peers, manager)

Has your learning had any impact on the organisation more widely, in what way?

In what ways has your learning been influenced by others?

Have changes in the organisation had any impact on you and the way you do your job, interact with others *etc.*?

The organisation

What do you understand by organisational learning?

In what ways do you see your organisation learn? Give me some examples. Where do you see organisational learning?

Where do you see organisational learning not happening. Give some examples of this.

In what ways has the organisation changed and adapted? How did you become aware of this change?

Development Event Interview: Line Managers

Preparation

How were you involved in the development event prior to your subordinate attending (*ie* did you recommend it, did you have experience of it yourself)?

What preparation were you involved in before your subordinates attended the programme?

What were you told officially/by others?

What did you hope they would get out of the course? What did you fear, what did you expect?

Were you asked to write anything/complete any tests/gather any information?

Did you talk to your subordinates before they attended the course, what was the substance of this?

Impact

Did you discuss the event with them when they returned. In what way?

In what ways have they changed as a result of the development event? What has been the biggest change?

(Performance at work/knowledge they can bring to the job/relationship with you/peers/subordinates/confidence/interpersonal skills/self understanding)

What are they doing differently? (explore 2 or 3 critical incidents)

How have you been able to help with this process? What has your involvement been?

How has the impact of the course changed over time?

Explore if they have sufficient awareness:

What would you say was the most valuable aspects of the event?

What other features of the programme were important/had the biggest impact?

And those that you think should change?

What has been the response of those around? What has been the reaction to the event?

Have you been aware of any resistance/help with what was learned?

Has your organisation itself helped in any way? What has worked/what hasn't?

Has the organisation changed at all as a result of the event? In what ways.

Have you yourself experienced the same or similar development event, If so explore views *etc.* Has this helped/in what ways?

Development Event Interview: Subordinates

Preparation

Where you aware of your manager attending the development event? Where you told officially/by others?

Were you asked to write anything/complete any tests/gather any information, provide any feedback?

Impact

Did they discuss the event with you when they returned. In what way?

In what ways have they changed as a result of the development event? What has been the biggest change?

(performance at work/knowledge they can bring to the job/relationship with you/peers/own managers/confidence/interpersonal skills/self understanding)

What are they doing differently? (explore 2 or 3 critical incidents)

How have you been involved with this process?

How has the impact of the course changed over time?

What has been the response of those around? What has been the reaction to the event?

Have you been aware of any resistance/help with what was learned?

Have you learned anything as a result of this event? Has there been any impact on you?

Has your organisation itself helped in any way? What has worked/what hasn't?

Has the organisation changed at all as a result of the course? In what ways.

Have you yourself experienced the same or similar development event? If so explore views *etc.* Has this helped/in what ways?

Appendix 2: Bibliography

Argyris C, Schon D A (1974), *Theory in Practice*, Jossey Bass, San Francisco

Argyris C, Schon D A (1978), *Organizational Learning: A Theory of Action Perspective*, Addison-Wesley, Massachusetts

Argyris C, Schon D (1981), *Organizational Learning*, Addison-Wesley, Massachusetts

Argyris C (1991), 'Teaching Smart People How to Learn' *Harvard Business Review*, Vol. 9 (3)

Bartolome F (1989), 'Nobody Trusts the Boss Completely; Now What?', *Harvard Business Review*, Vol. 67

Bateson G (1987), *Steps to an Ecology of Mind*, Jason Aronson, San Francisco

Baldwin T T, Padgett M Y (1993), 'Management Development: A Review and Commentary' *International Review of Industrial and Organizational Psychology*, Vol. 8

Bourner T (1996), private correspondence

Campanelli P, Channell J (1994), *Training: An Exploration of the Word and the Concept with an Analysis of the Implications for Survey Design*, Employment Department Research Series No. 30

Constable J, McCormick R (1987), *The Making of British Managers*, BIM/CBI, London

Gallie D, White M (1993), *Employee Commitment and the Skills Revolution: First Findings from the Employment in Britain Survey*, PSI, London

Garvin D A (1993), 'Building a Learning Organization', *Harvard Business Review*, July-August

Greene M, Gibbons A (1991), 'Learning Logs for Self Development' *Training and Development*, February

The Institute for Employment Studies

Green F (1997), *Review of Information on the Benefits of Training for Employers*, DfEE Research Report No. 7

Guest D, MacKenzie-Davey (1995), 'The Learning Organisation: Hype or Help', Paper for the Careers Research Forum, March

Handy C (1987), *The Making of Managers*, MSC/NEDC/BIM, London

Harri-Augstein S, Thomas L (1991) *Learning Conversations: The Self Organised Learning Way to Personal and Organisational Growth*, Routledge, London

Hayes R H, Wheelwright S C, Clark K B (1988), *Dynamic Manufacturing: Creating the Learning Organization*, The Free Press, New York

Hirsh D, Wagner D (1993), *What Makes Workers Learn: The role of incentives in workbased training and education*, National Centre on Adult Literacy, Philadelphia

Hout T M, Carter J C (1993), 'Getting it Done: New Roles for Senior Executives', *Harvard Business Review*, November-December, 133-145

Jones A M, Hendry C (1994), 'The Learning Organisation Adult Learning and Organisational Transformation', *British Journal of Management*, Vol. 5

Kettley P, Strebler M (1997), *Changing Roles for Senior Managers*, IES Report 327

Kim D H (1993), 'The Link Between Individual and Organizational Learning', *Sloan Management Review*, Fall

Knowles M S (1989), 'Everything you wanted to know from Malcolm Knowles (and weren't afraid to ask)', *Training*, August

Kremer-Bennett J, O'Brien M J (1994), 'The Building Blocks of the Learning Organisation', *Training*, June

Lessem R (1994), *Total Quality Learning: Building a Learning Organisation*, Blackwell Business, Oxford

Megginson D (1994), 'Planned and Emergent Learning: A Framework and Method', *Executive Development*, Vol. 7, No. 6

Metcalf H, Walling A, Fogerty M (1994), *Individual Commitment to Learning; Employees' Attitudes*, DfEE Research Series No. 40

Mitrani A, Dalziel M, Fitt D (1992), *Competency Based Human Resources Management*, John Wiley and Sons, Chichester

Mumford A (1997), *How to Choose the Right Development Method*, Honey, Maidenhead

Nonaka I, Takeuchi H (1995), *The Knowledge Creating Company: how Japanese companies create the dynamics of innovation.* Oxford University Press, New York

Pedlar M, Boydell T, Burgoyne J (1988), *Learning Company Project Report,* Manpower Services Commission, Sheffield

Pedlar M, Burgoyne J, Boydell T (1991), *The Learning Company,* McGraw Hill, New York

Pettigrew A, Whipp R (1991), *Managing Change for Competitive Success,* Basil Blackwell, Oxford

Revans R (1982), *The Origins and Growth of Action Learning,* Chartwell Brett, Bickley Kent

Senge P (1990), *The Fifth Discipline, the Art and Practice of the Learning Organisation,* Doubleday, New York

Tamkin P, Hillage J (1997), *Individual Commitment to Learning: Motivation and Rewards,* DfEE Research Report RR11

Torbert W (1991), *The Power of Balance,* Sage, London

Torbert W (1994), 'Managerial Learning, Organisational Learning — a potentially powerful redundancy', *Management Learning,* Vol. 25, No. 1, pp. 57-70

Towers J (1995), *World Class Performance from World Class People,* address to the 1995 IES Annual Dinner

Tremlett N, Park A (1995), *Individual Commitment to Learning: Comparative Findings from the Surveys of Individuals', Employers' and Providers' Attitudes,* Employment Department (SCPR)

Vygotsky L S (eds Cole M, John-Steiner V, Scribner S, Souberman E) (1978), *Mind in Society,* Harvard University Press, Cambridge MA

Vygotsky L S (1988), *Thought and Language,* MIT Press